KEYSTONE TOMBSTONES

Biographies of Famous People Buried in Pennsylvania

Battle of Gettysburg

JOE FARRELL AND JOE FARLEY
WITH LAWRENCE KNORR

SUNBURY PRESS
Mechanicsburg, PA USA

Published by Sunbury Press, Inc.
Mechanicsburg, Pennsylvania

www.sunburypress.com

For information about special discounts for bulk purchases, please contact Sunbury Press Orders Dept. at (855) 338-8359 or orders@sunburypress.com.

To request one of our authors for speaking engagements or book signings, please contact Sunbury Press Publicity Dept. at publicity@sunburypress.com.

SECOND SUNBURY PRESS EDITION: October 2020

Set in Adobe Garamond | Interior design by Crystal Devine | Cover by Lawrence Knorr | Edited by the authors.

Publisher's Cataloging-in-Publication Data
Names: Farrell, Joe, author | Farley, Joe, author | Knorr, Lawrence, author.
Title: Keystone tombstones battle of gettysburg : biographies of famous people buried in pennsylvania / Joe Farrell, Joe Farley, and Lawrence Knorr.
Description: Second trade paperback edition. | Mechanicsburg, PA : Sunbury Press, 2020. | Includes biographical references and index.
Summary: Biographies of participants in the Battle of Gettysburg who are buried in Pennsylvania are featured in this special volume.
Identifiers: ISBN 978-1-620064-52-8 (softcover).
Subjects: HISTORY / US History / Civil War | BIOGRAPHY & AUTOBIOGRAPHY / Rich & Famous | HISTORY / US History / Mid-Atlantic.

Product of the United States of America
0 1 1 2 3 5 8 13 21 34 55

Continue the Enlightenment!

Contents

INTRODUCTION

by Lawrence Knorr

An Overview of the Battle of Gettysburg

Many historians point to the simultaneous Union victories at Gettysburg and Vicksburg as the Civil War's turning point. These historians can say that because they know what happened since. However, the people alive at the time had no idea this was such a watershed moment. Yes, the Mississippi River was now under Union control thanks to Grant at Vicksburg successfully executing a crucial part of Winfield Scott's Anaconda Plan to encircle, blockade, and choke off the South. But Gettysburg was another story. Indeed, the losses on both sides were greater than any other battle. Indeed, the Union could claim victory because Robert E. Lee's invasion of the North was repelled. But Lee was still in the field. Meade did not follow up despite the urging of many of his generals and President Lincoln. The war would last nearly two more years, with Lee providing the toughest fight for the South.

So, what of Gettysburg? Why is it the most visited battlefield in the country? So much has been written about it and the people who played their parts. Everyday places like a wheatfield and a peach orchard are now capitalized when used at Gettysburg because the actions occurring within them are now legendary. History has made the people and places involved larger than life. In many ways, the battle is alive within us and the Adams County community in which it happened. Tour guides speak of unit commanders and specific soldiers as if they knew them personally or were alive today, just over yonder, carrying on with the fight. This is what makes the Battle of Gettysburg great. It remains living history to thousands of enthusiasts and millions of tourists seeking an escape to an earlier, simpler time when the nation fought for its survival.

So, what happened at Gettysburg? Following is a summary of the battle to help put the following chapters into context.

Before the Battle

Robert E. Lee, the commanding general of the Confederate Army of Northern Virginia, invaded the North in June of 1863. Jefferson Davis, the President of the Confederate States of America, and his field commander both knew Vicksburg's fall was likely to happen. They knew if Lee took the fight to the North, farmers in Virginia could produce a season of crops rather than lose them to the foraging army. They knew the North was in a tenuous situation politically. Another Confederate victory might tip the scales and force the North to negotiate a settlement to preserve the Confederacy. Another victory might encourage France or England to side with them or offer to broker a peace treaty.

Lee led his army up the Shenandoah Valley and across the Potomac River into Maryland. By late June, his army had captured Chambersburg, Carlisle, Mechanicsburg, Hanover, and was threatening Harrisburg, the capital of Pennsylvania, the ultimate prize in his mind. If Pennsylvania's capital, the second largest state in the Union, fell to the Confederates, it would be a stunning blow.

Meanwhile, Lincoln was changing commanders, moving on from General Joe Hooker. He interviewed John Fulton Reynolds, who politely declined the position. Reynolds suggested Meade, who was also from Pennsylvania. Lincoln approached him, and Meade accepted. Thus, at the end of June, the Union army was to the South, protecting Washington, D.C., while Lee was in the North, threatening Harrisburg. Meade ordered his forces North to face Lee. Getting word of Northern movements that could potentially cut off his army from its supply lines, Lee ordered his forces to converge southward towards the approaching Federals. The two armies met at Gettysburg on July 1, 1863.

First Day: July 1, 1863

Confederates under A. P. Hill headed east on the Chambersburg Road towards Gettysburg. They were met by cavalry under Union General John Buford, a subordinate to Major General John Reynolds. Buford stalled the Confederates, who were soon joined by Richard Ewell's forces from the north. As Reynolds arrived late in the morning, he positioned the Union troops to defend Gettysburg to the north and west of town.

Tragically, Reynolds gave his life, and soon the Confederates were overwhelming the positions. The Union fell back to a line on Cemetery Hill, south of Gettysburg, along the Emmitsburg Road.

Second Day: July 2, 1863

During the second day, Lee's army attacked multiple fronts to attempt to break the Union lines, which had formed like a fishhook, bending north to south from Culp's Hill, past Cemetery Hill, along Cemetery Ridge, to the Peach Orchard and Little Roundtop.

At Culp's Hill, Ewell attacked Henry Slocum. At Cemetery Hill, Ewell also attacked Oliver Howard. A.P. Hill attacked Cemetery Ridge and Winfield Scott Hancock. However, the critical action was on the south flank where Longstreet attacked Dan Sickles at the Peach Orchard and Devil's Den, with his sites on Little Round Top. Had he taken that hill, the Confederates would have won critical high ground. Units under George Sykes, including Strong Vincent, Joshua Chamberlain, and Samuel Crawford, successfully fended Longstreet's men and held the hill.

Third Day: July 3, 1863

The Union consolidated its fishhook. On the third day, the Confederates attacked all fronts: Ewell on the northeast attacking Slocum and Howard, and Longstreet's men traversing the ground from Seminary Ridge to Cemetery Ridge, the most famous section of the attack known as Pickett's Charge. The Confederate attacks were again repulsed.

Lee's Retreat: July 5 through July 14

After briefly pausing to reorganize, the Confederates split their forces and moved west and southwest, converging on Waynesboro and Greencastle, Pennsylvania, before reaching Hagerstown, Maryland. They crossed the Potomac at Williamsport, Maryland, after being delayed by floods. The Union forces shadowed Lee, always protecting access to Washington, D.C. The Union forces harassed Lee but did not make a significant effort to confront Lee, potentially trapping him at Williamsport. Lee was safely back in what is now West Virginia by July 14.

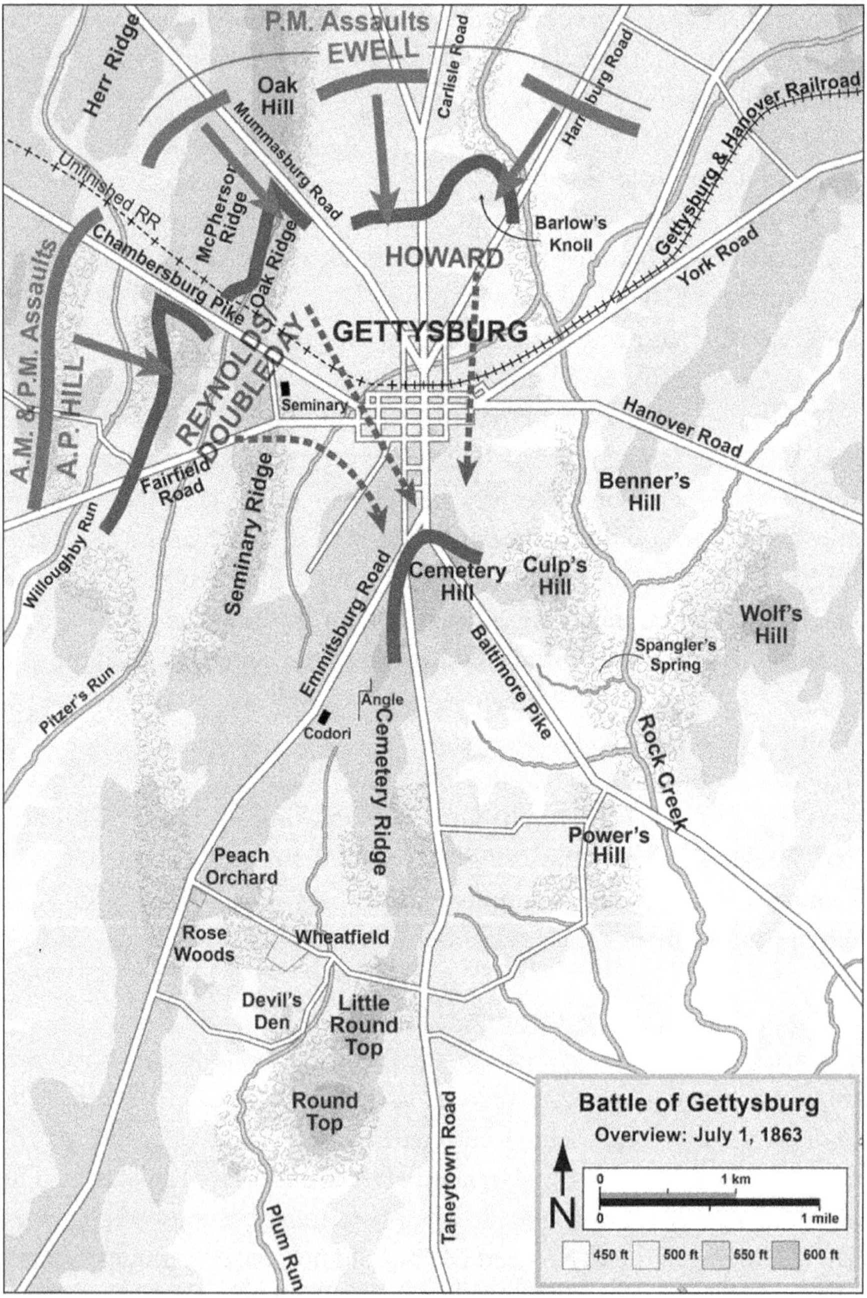
P.M. Assaults
EWELL
Herr Ridge
Oak Hill
Mummasburg Road
Carlisle Road
Harrisburg Road
Gettysburg & Hanover Railroad
Unfinished RR
McPherson Ridge
Oak Ridge
Chambersburg Pike
Barlow's Knoll
HOWARD
York Road
A.M. & P.M. Assaults
A.P. HILL
REYNOLDS
DOUBLEDAY
GETTYSBURG
Seminary
Hanover Road
Fairfield Road
Seminary Ridge
Benner's Hill
Willoughby Run
Emmitsburg Road
Cemetery Hill
Culp's Hill
Wolf's Hill
Baltimore Pike
Spangler's Spring
Pitzer's Run
Angle
Codori
Cemetery Ridge
Rock Creek
Power's Hill
Peach Orchard
Rose Woods
Wheatfield
Devil's Den
Little Round Top
Round Top
Taneytown Road
Plum Run
Battle of Gettysburg
Overview: July 1, 1863
N
0
1 km
0
1 mile
450 ft
500 ft
550 ft
600 ft

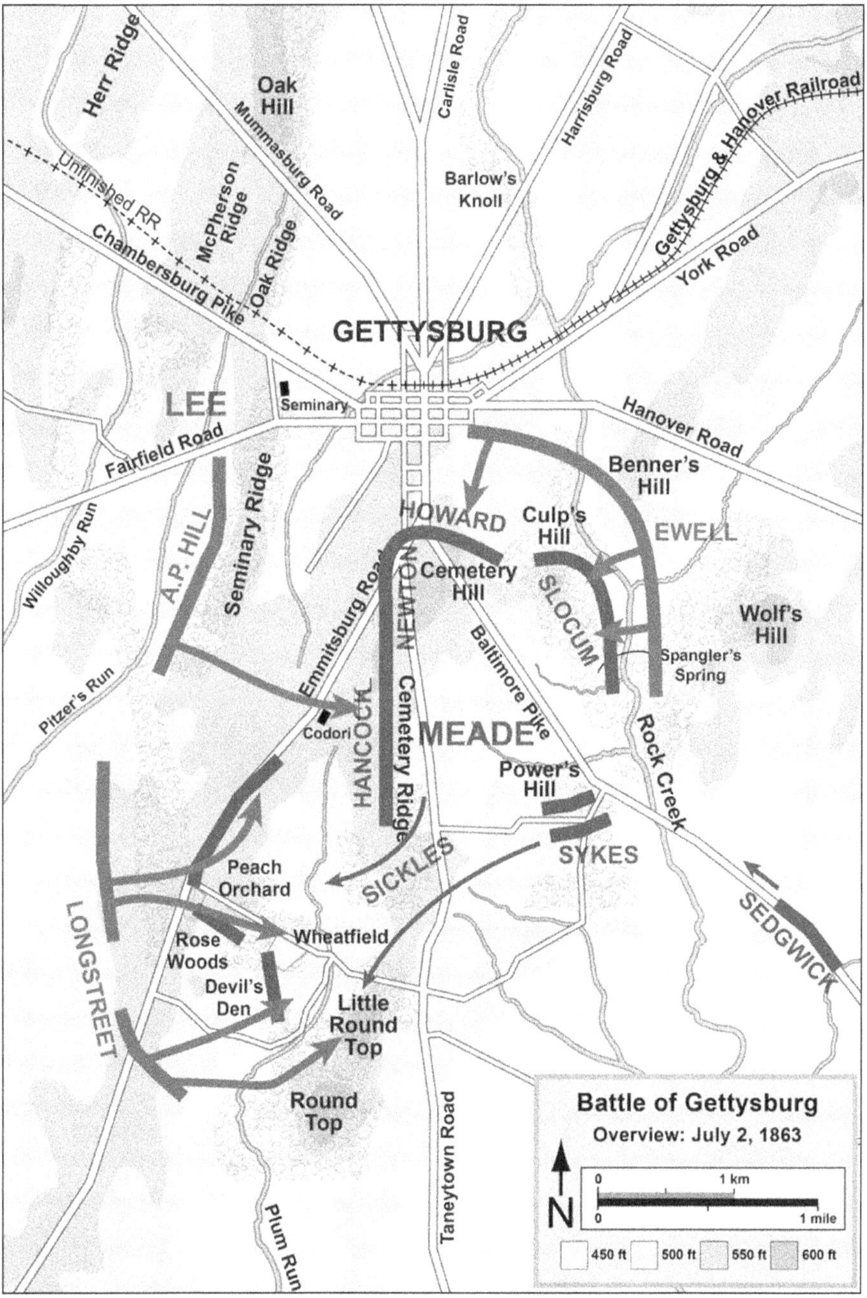

Herr Ridge
Oak Hill
Mummasburg Road
Carlisle Road
Harrisburg Road
Gettysburg & Hanover Railroad
Unfinished RR
McPherson Ridge
Oak Ridge
Chambersburg Pike
Barlow's Knoll
York Road
GETTYSBURG
Seminary
LEE
Fairfield Road
Hanover Road
Benner's Hill
Seminary Ridge
A.P. HILL
Willoughby Run
HOWARD
Culp's Hill
EWELL
Cemetery Hill
NEWTON
SLOCUM
Wolf's Hill
Emmitsburg Road
Baltimore Pike
Spangler's Spring
Pitzer's Run
HANCOCK
Cemetery Ridge
Codori
MEADE
Rock Creek
Power's Hill
SYKES
SICKLES
Peach Orchard
SEDGWICK
LONGSTREET
Rose Woods
Wheatfield
Devil's Den
Little Round Top
Round Top
Taneytown Road
Plum Run
Battle of Gettysburg
Overview: July 2, 1863
N
0
1 km
0
1 mile
450 ft
500 ft
550 ft
600 ft

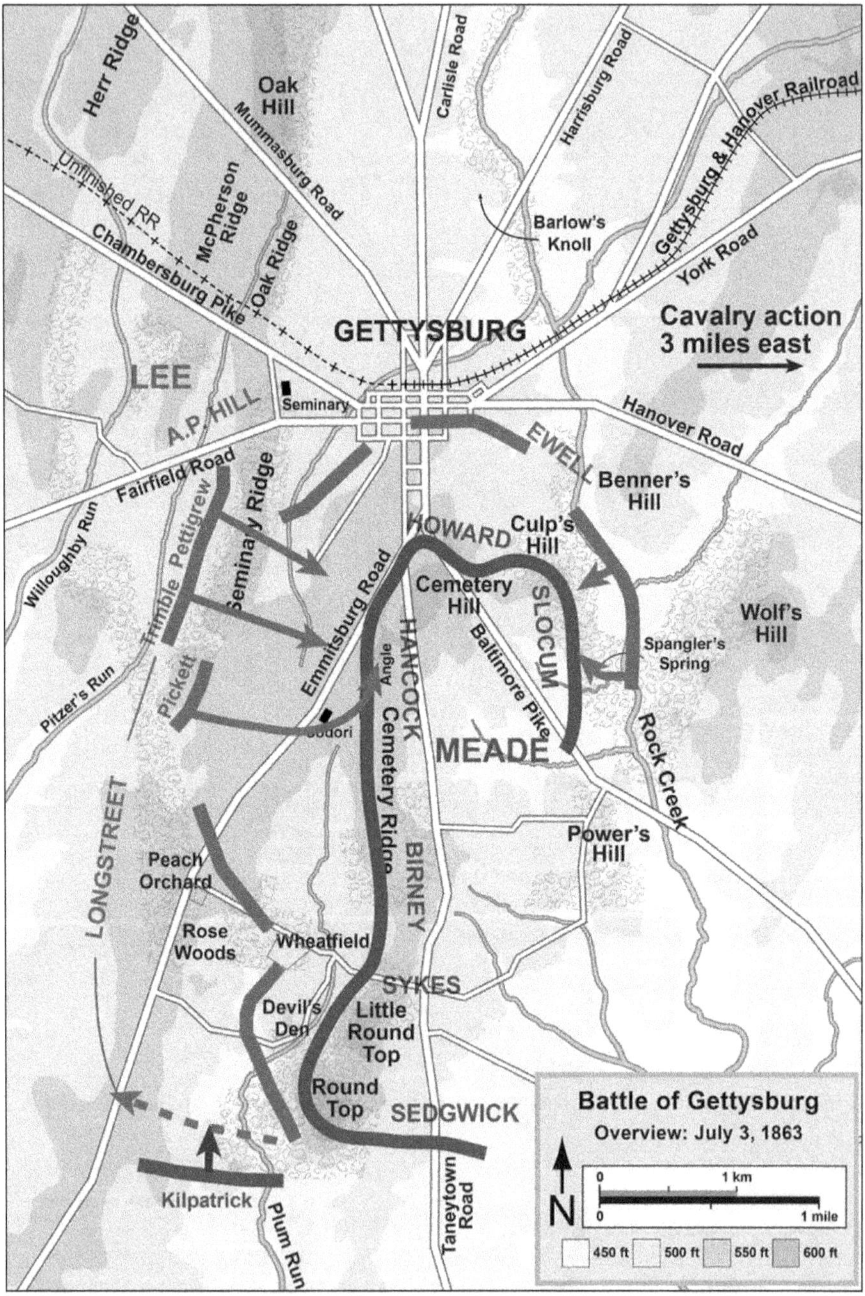
Herr Ridge
Oak Hill
Mummasburg Road
Carlisle Road
Harrisburg Road
Gettysburg & Hanover Railroad
Unfinished RR
McPherson Ridge
Oak Ridge
Chambersburg Pike
Barlow's Knoll
York Road
GETTYSBURG
Cavalry action 3 miles east
LEE
Seminary
A.P. HILL
Hanover Road
EWELL
Fairfield Road
Benner's Hill
Seminary Ridge
Pettigrew
Trimble
Willoughby Run
HOWARD
Culp's Hill
Cemetery Hill
SLOCUM
Wolf's Hill
Emmitsburg Road
Angle
HANCOCK
Baltimore Pike
Spangler's Spring
Pitzer's Run
Pickett
Codori
Cemetery Ridge
MEADE
Rock Creek
LONGSTREET
Power's Hill
Peach Orchard
BIRNEY
Rose Woods
Wheatfield
SYKES
Devil's Den
Little Round Top
Round Top
SEDGWICK
Kilpatrick
Plum Run
Taneytown Road
Battle of Gettysburg
Overview: July 3, 1863
N
0
1 km
0
1 mile
450 ft
500 ft
550 ft
600 ft

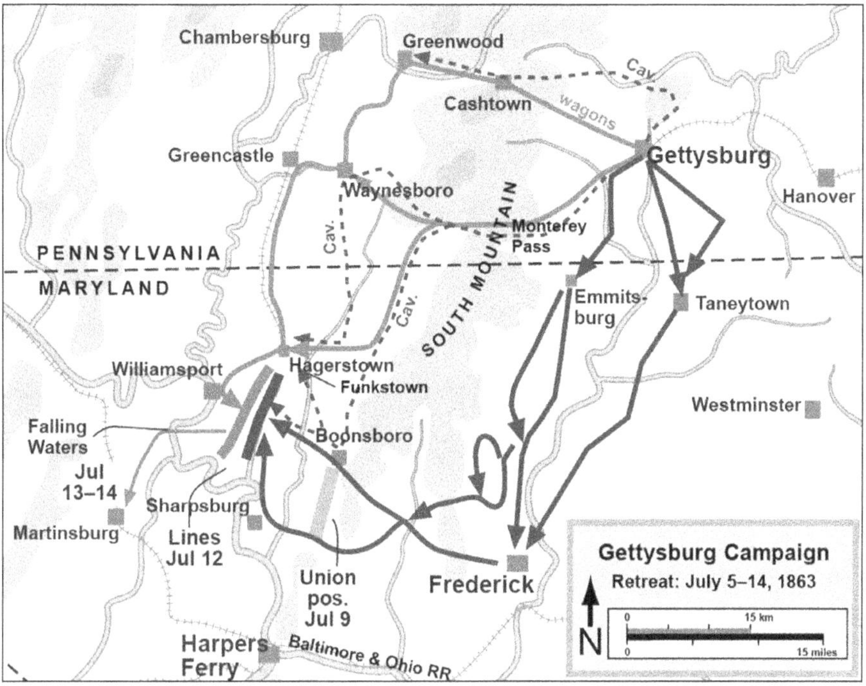

Throughout the rest of this book, you will find biographies of those who played a part at the Battle of Gettysburg and are buried somewhere in Pennsylvania. Some gave their lives during those three days in July. Others are veterans of the battle who lived to tell their tales. Included are major generals, noteworthy soldiers of various ranks, and even ordinary citizens. Also included is a chapter about the terrible price paid at Gettysburg and the subsequent visit by Abraham Lincoln to dedicate the cemetery. Lastly, some Confederates who never made it home and are buried on Pennsylvania soil are mentioned.

It should be noted, through a twist of fate, both Union victories at Vicksburg and Gettysburg ended on July 4, 1863, Independence Day. Lee began his retreat that day, and General Pemberton surrendered in Mississippi. As we now know, this turned the tide, and the Confederates were on the defensive for the rest of the war.

I.

GENERAL JOHN FULTON REYNOLDS

A True American Hero

County: Lancaster • Town: Lancaster
Buried at Lancaster Cemetery
205 East Lemon Street

John Reynolds gave his life for his country during the Battle of Gettysburg. He was one of the Union Army's most respected senior commanders. He fought in the Battles of Second Bull Run, Fredericksburg, Chancellorsville, and Gettysburg. He was captured in June 1862 and held prisoner at the infamous Libby Prison in Richmond. Within two months, Reynolds was exchanged for Lloyd Tilghman, a Confederate general who was later killed at the Battle of Champion Hill. President Lincoln offered Reynolds command of the entire Army of the Potomac, but he turned it down because he thought he would not be given a free hand. It was Reynolds's opinion that previous commanders had become bogged down due to political influences.

John Reynolds was born in Lancaster, Pennsylvania, on September 20, 1820. He was one of nine children. Two of his brothers would also go on to have distinguished military careers. He was educated in local schools. The future President, Senator James Buchanan, nominated Reynolds to attend the United States Military Academy in 1837. He graduated in 1841, 26th in a class of 50.

Reynolds experienced his first real military action during the Mexican War. During the war, he served under General Zachary Taylor and performed quite well. He received two promotions during the conflict. Reynolds was made a captain as a result of his gallantry during

John Fulton Reynolds

the Battle of Monterrey. During the Battle of Buena Vista, his unit prevented the Mexican Army from outflanking the Americans. This earned him the rank of major. During this conflict, he befriended both Winfield Scott Hancock and Lewis A. Armistead. Hancock would be a fellow Union officer at Gettysburg, where he would be wounded. Armistead would fight on the Confederate side, and be killed on the third day of the battle at the high point of the Confederate advance during Pickett's Charge.

This monument marks the spot where Reynolds fell on the initial day of the Battle of Gettysburg.

After the Mexican War, Reynolds remained in the Army. He was stationed in Oregon, and he took part in the 1857 Utah War with the Mormons. Returning east, he became the Commandant of Cadets at West point from 1860-1861. Here he trained men, some of whom fought on the Union side, and some who rallied to the Confederacy during the Civil War.

Shortly after the War between the States began, Reynolds was promoted to the rank of brigadier general. Major General George McClellan took steps to see to it that Reynolds was assigned to the just-created Army of the Potomac. He was put in charge of a brigade of Pennsylvania volunteers.

The first major battle he fought in was the Battle of Beaver Creek Dam. The Confederates launched a major attack on June 26, 1862, but Reynolds held his position. The Confederates attacked the next day again. Reynolds had gone 48 hours without sleep. Believing he was safe, he found a place to get some rest. The Union's retreating troops left him behind, and he was captured. The Confederates who captured him brought him before their general, D. H. Hill. Hill and Reynolds were friends from before the war, and Hill told Reynolds not to feel bad, that this is what happened in wars. As detailed earlier, the Union quickly arranged a prisoner exchange that resulted in Reynolds's release.

Reynolds, upon his release, quickly distinguished himself on the field of battle. On the second day of the Second Battle of Bull Run, the Union Army was disorganized and in a mass retreat. Reynolds led his men in a risky counterattack. It proved a success, giving the Union Army time to regroup and retreat in an orderly fashion. Some believe

THE FALL OF REYNOLDS.

Monument honoring John Reynolds on the Gettysburg battlefield.

that without Reynolds, the Union troops may have been totally defeated that day.

The Battle of Chancellorsville took place in May of 1863 and resulted in a major Union defeat. Reynolds was highly upset with the Commander of the Army at the time, Major General Hooker. After being overrun by a Stonewall Jackson flank attack, Hooker called his generals together. Three of the five generals urged Hooker to stay on the offensive, but he decided to retreat. Reynolds said in a manner that he intended Hooker to hear, "What was the use of calling us together at this time of night when he intended to retreat anyhow?"

Reynolds's final appearance on the field of battle was at Gettysburg. Brigadier General John Buford, a Union Cavalry officer, arrived in the small Pennsylvania town first. He occupied the town and set up defensive lines outside of town on high ground that he believed ideal to repel attacks. When General Buford decided to try to hold the high ground on Day 1 of the Battle of Gettysburg, he did so partly because it was John Reynolds who was supposed to arrive with his infantry. He respected Reynolds and believed he would arrive in time to relieve his cavalry troops. Buford did hold the ground for Reynolds, who arrived as fighting was underway. After a conference with Buford, Reynolds led his soldiers to the front lines and was putting them in place when he was downed by a shot, from what most believe was a Confederate sniper. He died instantly, and his command was assumed by Major General Abner Doubleday, who would become famous for allegedly creating America's national pastime.

Reynolds was the first and highest-ranking general to die at Gettysburg. His men loved him, and historian Shelby Foote wrote

JOHN FULTON REYNOLDS
COLONEL OF THE FIFTH INFANTRY, U.S. ARMY
MAJOR GENERAL OF VOLUNTEERS
BORN SEPTEMBER 21, 1820
KILLED AT THE BATTLE OF GETTYSBURG
WHILE COMMANDING THE
LEFT WING OF THE ARMY OF THE POTOMAC
JULY 1, 1863

Base of monument marking the grave of General John Reynolds in Lancaster

that many considered him the best general in the army. His body was transported to Lancaster, where he was buried on July 4, 1863. He was only 42.

Reynolds was so important to the Union effort and so highly thought of that he is memorialized by three statues in Gettysburg National Park (McPherson Ridge, The National Cemetery, and the Pennsylvania Memorial). There is also a statue of Reynolds in front of the Philadelphia City Hall.

A monument marks the spot on the Gettysburg battlefield where Reynolds fell. His grave is in Lancaster Cemetery near the entrance and one of the best kept in the old cemetery.

If You Go:

There are several other Civil War veterans' graves in Lancaster Cemetery, including John Reynolds's older brother, Rear Admiral William Reynolds, who served as commander on the USS *New Hampshire* in the Union Navy's blockade of the Southern ports. Two brevet brigadier generals, Henry Hambright and Samuel Ross, are also buried there as well as Colonel David Miles, who was captured at the Battle of Chickamauga and confined to Libby Prison. He successfully escaped and returned to Union army, where he led a brigade in Sherman's March to the Sea. Also, President James Buchanan, who was instrumental in getting Reynolds accepted to West Point, is buried in Lancaster. The former president (see *Keystone Tombstones Civil War* Chapter 1) is buried in Woodland Hill Cemetery. Visitors to Lancaster may also want to check out *Keystone Tombstones Volume 1* Chapter 21, on Thomas Mifflin.

2.

GEORGE G. MEADE

The Old Snapping Turtle

County: Philadelphia • Town: Philadelphia
Buried at Laurel Hill Cemetery
3822 Ridge Avenue

George Gordon Meade was a career United States Army officer and is best known for being the victor of the Battle of Gettysburg in 1863. He was born on December 31, 1815, in Spain. His father was serving there as an agent for the United States Government. In 1828, his father died, and six months later, the family, facing financial difficulties, returned to the United States. Initially, George was educated at the Mount Hope Institution in Baltimore. In 1831, with financial considerations being a prime consideration, he entered the United States Military Academy at West Point. He graduated ranked nineteenth in his class of 56 cadets in 1835 and was transferred to Florida at the beginning of the Seminole Wars. He became ill with a fever in Florida and was reassigned to Massachusetts. He was very disillusioned with the military and resigned his commission in 1836. He went to work for a railroad company as an engineer to survey territory for new rail lines.

In 1840 he met Margaretta Sergeant, and soon she became his wife. She was the daughter of John Sergeant, who was Henry Clay's running mate in the 1832 presidential election. They had seven children together. With a family to support, Meade found it difficult to secure steady employment. Though he had never intended to make the army a career, he reapplied to the military in 1842 and was appointed a 2nd lieutenant in the Topographical Engineers. He was assigned to General Winfield Scott's army during the War with Mexico. He was brevetted to first lieutenant as a result of his conduct during the Battle of Monterrey.

George Gordon Meade

After the war in Mexico, Meade moved back to Philadelphia, where he worked on building lighthouses for the Delaware Bay. He was eventually promoted to captain, and for the next ten years, he spent time in surveying and design work for lighthouses on the east coast. He oversaw the construction of lighthouses at Barnegat, Atlantic City, and Cape May, New Jersey. Among his accomplishments during this period was the design of a hydraulic lamp that was approved by the Lighthouse Board for use in American lighthouses. He also participated in the survey of the Great Lakes and tributaries.

He was promoted from captain to brigadier general in August 1861, just a few months after the start of the Civil War. The sectional strife took a personal toll on the Meades as his wife's sister was married to Governor Wise of Virginia, who became a brigadier general in the Confederate Army. Nicknamed "The Old Snapping Turtle," Meade gained a reputation for being short-tempered and obstinate. In March 1862, he was severely wounded at the Battle of Glendale. A musket ball struck him above his hip, clipped his liver, and just missed his spine as it passed through his body. He recovered from his wounds in Philadelphia and led his brigade at the Battle of Second Bull Run and the Battles of South Mountain, Antietam, and Fredericksburg. Soon after Fredericksburg, Meade was assigned to command the Fifth Army Corps of the Army of the Potomac. His assignment as corps commander took him through the trial of the Battle of Chancellorsville in May 1863. Though the army had been soundly defeated there, Meade handled his corps with great skill and protected the important fords on the Rappahannock River.

Unhappy with the performance of the Army of the Potomac, President Lincoln changed command from McClellan to Burnside to Hooker, He offered the position to John Reynolds, but he refused. Next up was Meade, who assumed command just days before the monumental Battle of Gettysburg, which is considered the turning point of the war. In defending his decision to appoint Meade as commander of the Union forces, Lincoln said, "Meade will fight well on his own dunghill."

Meade was fortunate to have such competent and brave officers as Reynolds, Buford, Hancock, Vincent, Custer, and Chamberlain with him

General Meade's monument at Gettysburg

at Gettysburg. Meade decided to fight a defensive battle and did well in deploying his forces. His forces repelled attacks on his flanks and, on the final day of the battle, stood tall against an attack on the center of their lines. This disastrous attack became known as Pickett's Charge. Although Meade field-marshaled the Union victory at Gettysburg, he was criticized severely then and now for not pursuing the defeated Confederate forces after the battle. Meade infuriated Lincoln when he reported that the "invaders have been driven from our land." Reportedly, upon receiving the dispatch, Lincoln said angrily, "Doesn't he understand it's all our land?"

Lincoln was overwrought at the missed opportunity to perhaps end the war and ordered Meade to pursue and attack Lee's retreating army. It was too late, however, and Lee escaped to Virginia. In March, Lincoln put General Ulysses S. Grant in charge of all Union Armies.

When Grant was appointed, Meade offered his resignation. He wanted to allow Grant to appoint the general of his choosing for the position. Grant told Meade he had no intention of replacing him. While Meade stayed with the Army, he did not approve of Grant's tactics. Meade had become a cautious general while Grant was willing to attack and suffer losses, secure in the knowledge that he had replacements available, and the Confederates did not. By all accounts, Meade served Grant well during the remainder of the war. He received a promotion to major

Final resting place of George Meade "The Old Snapping Turtle" who commanded the victorious Union Army at Gettysburg

general at the war's end. He was outranked by only Grant, Halleck, and Sherman.

After the war, General Meade was a commissioner of Fairmont Park in Philadelphia from 1866 until his death. Before his death, he received an honorary doctorate in law from Harvard University. Also, his scientific achievements were recognized by several institutions, including the American Philosophical Society and the Academy of Natural Sciences of Philadelphia. He died on November 6, 1872, in the house where he lived at 1836 Delancey Place in Philadelphia, from complications of his old wounds combined with pneumonia. He was 56 years old. Many felt his victory at Gettysburg had stopped a rebel invasion of the city. After his death, his widow accepted the house as a gift from the city of Philadelphia. To this day, the house still has the word "Meade" over the door though now it has been converted into apartments. Meade is buried in a modest grave in Laurel Hill Cemetery in Philadelphia.

If You Go:

Laurel Hill is a large well-kept cemetery rich in history with many interesting graves. (See *Keystone Tombstones Volume 1* Chapter 12, on Harry Kalas). Once again, due to the size of this cemetery, if you visit, we advise you to make an initial stop at the cemetery office to obtain directions to the sites you are there to see.

Among the graves at Laurel Hill are three officers who fought with Meade at Gettysburg. Oliver Blatchy Knowles entered the war as a private and ended it as Brevet Brigadier General after fighting in Antietam, Shenandoah, Gettysburg, Spotsylvania, Petersburg, and the last campaign of Appomattox. He died less than two years after the war of cholera at the age of 25. William Lovering Curry fought at Gettysburg and was stationed at the famed "Copse of Trees" during Pickett's Charge. He was wounded at the Battle of Spotsylvania and died a month later. Alexander Williams Biddle fought at the Battles of Fredericksburg, Chancellorsville, Gettysburg, and Bristoe Station as a major and then lieutenant colonel.

Ulric Dahlgren was a Civil War army officer killed in a raid on Richmond in 1864. Papers found on him indicated he had orders to

Tombstone of Ulric Dahlgren, who was killed in a raid on Richmond, while carrying orders to assassinate Confederate President Jefferson Davis.

assassinate Confederate President Jefferson Davis and his Cabinet. The papers were published and created an enormous controversy (the Dahlgren Affair) in the following months and may have contributed to John Wilkes Booth's decision to assassinate Abraham Lincoln a year later.

Frank Furness served as a Civil War officer and was awarded the Congressional Medal of Honor for his bravery at Trevailian Station, Virginia. However, he was better known as a major architect from 1870 to 1890. He designed over 400 buildings, including banks, churches, synagogues, rail stations, and numerous mansions. His first major work, Philadelphia's Academy of Fine Arts, is still standing. His grave, however, is very modest and simple.

There are five other Civil War Congressional Medal of Honor recipients at Laurel Hill: Henry Harrison Bingham, George J. Pitman, John Hamilton Storey, Pinkerton Vaughn, and Robert Telford Kelly.

3.

WINFIELD S. HANCOCK

Hancock the Superb

County: Montgomery • Town: Norristown
Buried at Montgomery Cemetery
1 Hartranft Avenue

Winfield Scott Hancock was an American hero named after an American hero and given an appropriate and well-earned nickname, "Hancock the Superb." He was a career U.S. Army Officer, a hero in the Civil War, a commanding general at the Battle of Gettysburg, and the Democratic nominee for president in 1880.

Winfield Scott Hancock was born in Montgomery County, Pennsylvania, on Valentine's Day in 1824. He was named after General Winfield Scott, a hero in the War of 1812. Hancock was born with an identical twin brother named Hilary Booker Hancock. Hancock was educated at Norristown Academy at first but transferred to public schools in the late 1830s. In 1840, he was nominated to West Point by Congressman Joseph Fornance. He graduated in 1844, ranked eighteenth of twenty-five. He was commissioned a second lieutenant and assigned to the infantry.

When the Mexican War broke out in 1846, he was initially assigned to recruiting in Kentucky. He worked hard to get assigned to the front, but he was so successful as a recruiter, they were reluctant to let him go. He finally did get assigned to the front in July of 1847 in a regiment that made up part of the army led by General Winfield Scott. He was promoted to 1st lieutenant for "gallant and meritorious conduct" at the Battle of Churubusco, where he was wounded in the knee and developed a fever. The fever kept him from participating in the final breakthrough

Winfield Scott Hancock

at Mexico City much to his regret. He remained in Mexico until the peace treaty was signed in 1848.

After the Mexican War, he served in the West, in Florida, and elsewhere. It was while serving in St. Louis that he met Almira (Allie) Russell, whom he married in 1850. The couple had two children, Russell (1850–1884) and Ada (1857–1875). In 1855, he was promoted to captain, and in November 1858, he was stationed in southern California and joined by Almira and the children. There, Hancock became friends with several officers from the South and became especially close to Lewis Armistead of Virginia. At the outbreak of the Civil War, Armistead and other Southerners were leaving to join the Confederate Army, while Hancock was remaining in the U.S. Army.

On June 15, 1861, Hancock and Almira hosted a party for their friends who were scattered because of the war. The party has become a legend and is recounted in Michael Shaara's *The Killer Angels* and the movie *Gettysburg*. Armistead, who was widowed twice, had grown very close to the Hancocks and shed tears when it became time to end the party and depart. He gave some personal effects to Almira for safekeeping and promised he would not take arms against his friend, "Winnie." Almira said later that at the Battle of Gettysburg, Hancock's men killed three of the six Confederates who attended that party.

This monument marks the spot at Gettysburg where Hancock was wounded. The bullet that was removed from Hancock is preserved by the Montgomery County Historical Society.

Hancock headed east to assume quartermaster duties for a rapidly growing army, but on September 23, 1861, he was promoted to brigadier general and given command of an infantry brigade in the Amy of the Potomac. He took part in the Peninsula Campaign, and at the Battle of Williamsburg on May 5, 1862, he handled his troop so well that General George McClellan reported: "Hancock was superb." The epithet seemed to stick to him afterward, and "Hancock the Superb" was born.

He played a significant role at the Battle of Antietam and shortly afterward was promoted to Major

General of Volunteers in November 1862. He led his division in the disastrous attack on Marye's Heights in the Battle of Fredericksburg the following month, where he was wounded in the abdomen. He was wounded again at the Battle of Chancellorsville, covering General Hooker's withdrawal. On that day, General Darius Couch asked to be transferred out of the Army of the Potomac in protest of the actions of General Hooker. As a result, Hancock assumed command of 11 Corps, which he would lead until shortly before the war's end (General Couch had a long distinguished military career and has the remains of a fortification built to defend Harrisburg named after him in Lemoyne, Pennsylvania.).

Hancock's most famous service was at the Battle of Gettysburg during July 1–3, 1863. On the first day, after his friend Maj. Gen. John Reynolds (see Chapter 1) was killed, Gen. George Meade (see Chapter 2), the new commander of the Army of the Potomac, sent Hancock ahead to take command and to decide whether to continue to fight there or to fall back. He decided to stay, rallied his troops, and held Cemetery Ridge until the arrival of the main body of the Federal Army. During the second day's battle, he commanded the left-center and, after General Sickles had been wounded, the whole left wing. On the third day, he commanded the left-center and thus bore the brunt of Pickett's Charge. Hancock was shot in the groin while rallying and commanding his troops on horseback. Although severely wounded, he refused to be evacuated to the rear until the battle was resolved. During the battle, his old friend General Lewis Armistead was mortally wounded. As he lay dying, he asked to see Hancock. When told that Hancock could not come to see him because he had been wounded himself, Armistead asked that Hancock be told that he was sorry. Armistead died two days later, while Hancock took six months to recover enough to return to command. There is a monument on the Gettysburg Battlefield commemorating their friendship and another marking the spot where Armistead fell. Hancock was considered by many to have made the most impact by a general at Gettysburg. His courage in the face of fire and leadership played a huge role in the Union victory.

This is the Friend to Friend monument in the Gettysburg National Cemetery. The monument portrays the final moments in the life of Confederate General Lewis Armistead who died at Gettysburg and was close friends with General Hancock.

This monument on the Gettysburg battlefield marks the spot where Confederate General Lewis Armistead fell mortally wounded.

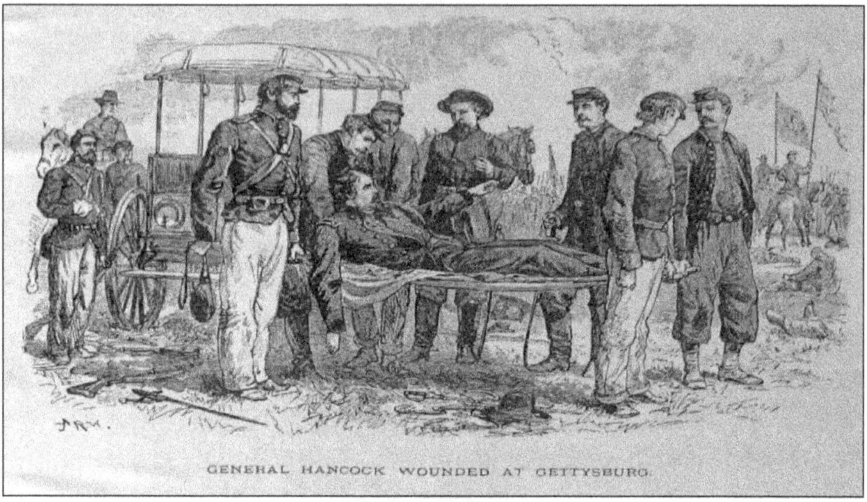
GENERAL HANCOCK WOUNDED AT GETTYSBURG.

This drawing of a wounded Hancock at Gettysburg is in the office at the Montgomery Cemetery.

Hancock suffered from the effects of his Gettysburg wound for the rest of the war. After recuperating in Norristown, he returned in March to the front and led his old corps under General Ulysses S. Grant in the 1864 Overland Campaign but was never quite his old self. He performed well at the Battle of the Wilderness, which began in May, and continued to fight at Yellow Tavern, North Anna, Old Church, Cold Harbor, Trevilian Station, and finally, the siege of Petersburg. In June, his Gettysburg wound reopened, but he soon resumed command, sometimes traveling by ambulance. After his corps participated in the assaults at Deep Bottom, Hancock was promoted to brigadier general in the Regular Army, effective August 12, 1864.

In Grant's campaign against Lee, Hancock and his famed 11 Corps were repeatedly called upon to plunge into the very worst of the fighting, and the casualties were terrible. The losses and lingering effects of his Gettysburg wound caused Hancock to give up field command in November 1864. He left the 11 Corps after a year in which it had suffered over 40,000 casualties but had achieved significant military victories. He was again promoted in March 1865 to brevet major general in the Regular Army.

After the assassination of Abraham Lincoln in April, Hancock was placed in charge of Washington, D.C., and it was under his command that John Wilkes Booth's accomplices were tried and executed. Hancock was reluctant to execute some of the less-culpable conspirators, especially Mary Surratt. He hoped Surratt would receive a pardon from President Johnson. He was so hopeful that he posted messengers from the arsenal, where the hangings took place, to the White House, ready to relay the news of a pardon to him, but no pardon was forthcoming. Afterward, he wrote that "every soldier was bound to act as I did under similar circumstances."

Hancock remained in the postwar army, and in 1866 Grant had him promoted to major general in the Regular Army, and he served at that rank for the rest of his life. He served briefly in the West and then was named military governor of Louisiana during Reconstruction. His policies there angered Republicans and Grant but made him popular among Democrats. When Grant won the presidency in 1868, Hancock found himself transferred to the Department of Dakota, which covered Minnesota, Montana, and the Dakotas. It was during this tour that Hancock contributed to the creation of Yellowstone National Park and had a summit (Mt. Hancock) at the southern boundary named in his honor.

With the death of General George Meade in 1872, Hancock became the senior major general in the U.S. Army and was assigned to take Meade's place as commander of the Division of the Atlantic at Governor's Island in New York Harbor.

Hancock had been considered as a presidential nominee by the Democrats as early as 1864. In 1880, he was finally chosen at the convention in Cincinnati, along with William Hayden English of Indiana as his running mate. They ran against James Garfield and Chester Arthur in an election that was very close in the popular vote, but not so close in the electoral. Garfield won by less than 10,000 votes but won the electoral vote 214 to 155. Garfield was assassinated in September 1881.

Hancock finished his life as Commander of the Division of the Atlantic and died at Governor's Island from an infected carbuncle complicated by diabetes on February 9, 1886. After a funeral in New York City, General Hancock's remains were taken to his boyhood home of Norristown, Pennsylvania, and placed with his daughter Ada in a mausoleum that he had designed.

Winfield Scott Hancock is memorialized three times at Gettysburg: once in a statue on Cemetery Hill, once on a statue as part of the Pennsylvania Memorial, and as a sculpture on the New York State Monument. There are statues in Washington, D.C., at Pennsylvania Avenue and 7th Street N.W. and in Fairmont Park in Philadelphia and a bronze bust in Hancock Square, New York City. His portrait adorns U.S. currency on the $2 silver certificate series of 1886 and is quite valuable today.

Actor Brian Mallon portrayed Hancock in two films about the Civil War: *Gettysburg* (1993) and *Gods and Generals* (2003). He is portrayed very favorably in both films. There are numerous books about Hancock, the most notable is *Winfield Scott Hancock: A Soldier's Life,* written by David M. Jordan and published in 1998.

Here is the grave of one of the greatest Union Civil War generals.

If You Go:

There are a few other interesting graves in Montgomery Cemetery. The most notable is the grave of John Frederick Hartranft, who is the subject of chapter 8 in this volume. Hartranft was awarded the Congressional Medal of Honor for his actions at the first Battle of Manassas. He rose to the rank of brigadier general and, after the war, was appointed a special provost marshall during the trial of those accused in President Lincoln's assassination. He led the convicted parties to the gallows and read them their last rites before they were hanged.

Returning to civilian life, he served as auditor general of Pennsylvania in John White Geary's (see *Keystone Tombstones Volume One* Chapter 9) administration before being elected governor in 1872. He was governor on the Day of the Rope, June 21, 1877, when ten Molly Maguires were hanged (see *Keystone Tombstones Volume One* Chapter 13).

Also buried in Montgomery Cemetery with Hancock is Brigadier General Samuel Kosciuszko Zook who fought with him at Gettysburg and was fatally wounded on the second day, and Brigadier General Adam Jacoby Slemmer who ignored pressure by the Confederates to surrender his command at Fort Barrancas, Florida, in 1861, instead moving it to Fort Pickens, Santa Rosa Island. This move ensured Union control of the Gulf of Mexico throughout the war.

Nearby Montgomery Cemetery at Lower Providence Presbyterian Church Cemetery in Eagleville lies the body of Civil War Congressional Medal of Honor recipient Hillary Beyer. He was awarded his Medal of Honor for his bravery at the Battle of Antietam, Maryland, in September 1862.

We were hungry and thirsty after our visit to Norristown and found a great place just down the road from Lower Providence Presbyterian Church at 3300 Ridge Pike. It's called Brother Paul's and had a great menu and service. You can sit inside or outside and choose from many delicious sounding items on the menu. We both loved our sandwiches. There were many options for wetting your whistle too. While we were waiting for our food, we loved taking in the décor. There were many great photographs throughout the large bar and dining areas. We even got to meet one of the Pauls himself. The Pauls are brothers-in-law, so we found out. He seemed like a fine American, so we asked if he might have us back for a book signing some evening. It looks like a fun place to have a pint or two. We're hoping he says, "yes."

Here are the Joes at Brothers Pauls refreshing ourselves after visiting Montgomery Cemetery. We hope to get back to visit the brothers in the future.

4.

JOHN BURNS

The Hero of Gettysburg

County: Adams • Town: Gettysburg
Buried at Evergreen Cemetery
799 Baltimore Street

On July 1, 1863, soldiers of the 7th Wisconsin Infantry and the 24th Michigan Infantry were stunned to see an elderly man dressed in dark trousers and a blue swallowtail coat with brass buttons and a high black silk hat join them in McPherson's Woods to await an attack by Confederate troops. He fought beside these men of the famous Iron Brigade throughout the afternoon, in one case shooting a charging Confederate officer from his horse.

His name was John Burns. Burns was born on September 5, 1793, in Burlington, New Jersey. He was a veteran of the War of 1812, where he served as an enlisted man and fought in numerous battles. In 1846, when war broke out with Mexico, Burns was one of the first to volunteer. He also served with valor in that conflict. When the Civil War began, he was 67 years old, but he immediately volunteered to serve in the Union army. He was rejected due to his advanced age. Though rejected for combat duty, he was permitted to serve the army as a teamster. However, within a short time, he was sent home to Gettysburg. Little did he realize, at the time, that this would allow him to fight.

Confederates rode into Gettysburg on June 26. During General Jubal Early's brief occupation of Gettysburg, Burns was the local constable. The rebels had him jailed for his adamant resistance and assertion of civil authority. As Confederate troops were leaving for Harrisburg, he was released from jail, and he promptly arrested some of the Confederate

John Burns

stragglers. He held them in custody until the arrival of Federal cavalry under Brigadier General John Buford on June 30.

The next day, when major combat erupted, Burns calmly took up his flintlock musket and walked out to the scene of the fighting. On his way, he encountered a wounded Union soldier and asked if he could borrow his more modern rifle for the battle. The soldier agreed, and Burns moved on, putting cartridges in his pockets. He ran into Major Thomas Chamberlin of the 150th Pennsylvania Infantry and asked to be allowed to fight with the regiment. Chamberlin referred him to the regimental commander, Colonel Langhorne Wister, who agreed to let him fight. Burns was wounded three times, and when the Union forces fell back under Confederate pressure, the Union soldiers were forced to leave

This monument sits on the Gettysburg battlefield near where Burns took his spot beside Union troops.

him behind. Although wounded and exhausted, he was able to crawl away from his rifle and bury his ammunition so that when captured by Confederates, he could claim he was a noncombatant. He succeeded in convincing the Confederates of such, and their surgeons treated his wounds in the arm, leg, and breast. Had Burns not convinced his captors, he would have been subject to summary execution as a non-uniformed combatant.

After the battle, Burns became a national hero. Matthew Brady's photographer, Timothy O'Sullivan, snapped a picture of Burns recuperating from his wounds and took the story back home to Washington. The alleged inventor of baseball, Major Abner Doubleday, called Burns "the Hero of Gettysburg." When President Lincoln came to Gettysburg a few months later to dedicate the Soldiers National Cemetery, it was John Burns he wanted to meet. President Lincoln and Burns walked together from David Will's house to the Presbyterian Church on Baltimore Street. Lincoln extended his thanks to John Burns on their walk. His fame spread all across the nation, and in 1864, the famous poet Bret Harte published a poem about Burn's exploits called "John Burns of Gettysburg," and Congress passed a special act granting him a pension.

In the last few years of his life, Burns had dementia. He would often wander from his home. He somehow found his way to New York City, where on a winter's night in December 1871, he was discovered in a state of destitution. He was sent home to Gettysburg, where he died of pneumonia on February 4, 1872. He was 78 years old.

A monument depicting a defiant Burns carrying his rifle and with a clenched fist can be found on McPherson's Ridge near where Burns fought with the Iron Brigade. The monument was dedicated on July 1, 1903, the 40th anniversary of the battle. Burns is buried in historic Evergreen Cemetery in Gettysburg. His grave is one of only two there with permission to fly the American flag twenty-four hours a day. The other grave is Ginnie Wade (see Chapter 13). A full-length biography titled *John Burns: The Hero of Gettysburg* by Timothy H. Smith was published in 2000.

If You Go:

Gettysburg is a fantastic town steeped in history. There is so much to see and do that we can only scratch the surface here. In the historic Evergreen Cemetery are many interesting graves, including those of Ginnie Wade and Hall of Fame baseball player Eddie Plank. Nearby Gettysburg National Cemetery is perhaps the most hallowed ground in our country and a sight to behold. It is the site of Lincoln's famous Gettysburg Address and the graves of 3512 Union soldiers, of which 979 are unknown.

Among those buried there are:

• **Amos Humiston** is the only individual enlisted man at Gettysburg who has a monument on the battlefield. Humiston was killed on July 1, 1863, the first day of the battle. When his body was discovered later that week, he was holding an ambrotype (an early kind of photograph) of three small children. There was nothing else to identify him, and the few soldiers from his unit, Company C, 154th New York Volunteer Infantry, who survived had moved on before he was found. Efforts to discover his identity using the picture started with a story in the *Philadelphia Inquirer* with the headline, "Whose Father is He?" The story swept the North, and his widow saw the photograph in a magazine and realized that her devoted husband was dead. The family was living in Portville, New York, and Amos had been dead for four months. The outpouring of sympathy was so great that the proceeds from fundraising allowed for the creation of an orphanage in Gettysburg for children of soldiers. Amos Humiston is buried in the New York Section of the National Cemetery, and his monument is on Stratton Street between York Street and the railroad, beside the fire station. See more details in the next chapter.

• **Cyrus James** is also buried in the New York plot. He is believed to be the first soldier killed in this famous and monumental battle. Ewell's forces, arriving from Cumberland County, killed him in a skirmish north of town before the main engagement.

Amos Humiston is the only enlisted man to have his own monument on the Gettysburg battlefield.

The tombstone of Charles Collis a Medal of Honor recipient for his actions during the battle of Fredericksburg. The men who served under him erected this monument.

• **Charles Henry Tucky Collis** was awarded the Congressional Medal of Honor for his bravery at the Battle of Fredericksburg on December 13, 1862. He survived the war and has an impressive grave in the National Cemetery.

• **William E. Miller**, of Cumberland County, was awarded the Congressional Medal of Honor for his bravery on the third day of the Battle of Gettysburg. He is buried in the Officer's Section in the National Cemetery.

• **George Nixon** was wounded during the second day of the Battle of Gettysburg. That night, as he lay on the battlefield between Union and Confederate lines, he cried out in pain. Musician Richard Enderlin crawled out and dragged Private Nixon most of the way back to safety then dashed the rest of the way with Nixon in tow. For this act, Enderlin was promoted to sergeant and awarded the Medal of Honor. Nixon's wounds were mortal, and he died in a hospital seven days later. He was the great-grandfather of Richard Nixon, our 37th president. His grave is in the Ohio plot.

5.

AMOS HUMISTON

A Moving Story of a Father's Love

County: Adams • Town: Gettysburg
Buried at Gettysburg National Cemetery
97 Taneytown Road

The Gettysburg Battlefield is full of monuments. Hundreds of monuments commemorate the men who led the soldiers in this epic battle for the nation's soul. There are monuments to states, divisions, brigades, and companies. There are monuments to generals and officers and even civilians, but what about enlisted men? There is but one enlisted man who has his monument on the battlefield at Gettysburg, and that man is Amos Humiston.

Sergeant Amos Humiston of the 154th New York Volunteer Infantry was killed on the first day of fighting at Gettysburg. Months earlier, Humiston's wife had mailed him an ambrotype (an early type of photograph) in which the couple's three children were pictured: Frank (age 8), Alice (6), and Freddie (4). After Humiston was killed, his body was found by a local Gettysburg girl, the daughter of a tavern-keeper, in a secluded spot at York and Stratton Streets. Humiston was clutching the photograph, which, as it turned out, was the only thing found on his person that could be used to identify him.

The girl gave the picture to her father, Benjamin Schriver. It became a conversation piece at his tavern. A physician named Dr. John Francis Bourns was in Gettysburg from Philadelphia to care for the wounded and was touched by the story when he visited Schriver's Tavern. He was so moved by the story of the soldier found holding the picture that he convinced Schriver to give him the picture so that he could try to locate

Ambrotype of Amos Humiston—the only known picture of him.

the dead man's family. Dr. Bourns saw to it that the soldier's grave was well marked and returned to Philadelphia with a plan.

On October 19, 1863, the *Philadelphia Inquirer* published a story under the headline: "Whose Father Was He?" The article began by describing the final act: "How touching! How solemn! What pen can describe the emotions of this patriot-father as he gazed upon these children, so soon to be made orphans!" The column continued with a detailed description of each of the children's physical appearances, as shown in the picture, which was necessary because newspapers of the time could not print photographs. The article gave Dr. Bourns's address and a request for newspapers throughout the country to spread the story:

The Humiston children. This photo was used to help identify their father, a Gettysburg casualty.

> "It is earnestly desired that all the papers in the country will draw attention to the discovery of this picture and its attendant circumstances, so that, if possible, the family of the dead hero may come into possession of it. Of what inestimable value will it be to these children, proving, as it does, that the last thoughts of their dying father was for them, and them only."

On October 29, 1863, a reprint of the *Inquirer's* article was published in the *American Presbyterian*, a church magazine. That is where Philinda Humiston of Portville, New York, a small town on the Allegheny River, saw the article and—having last received word from her husband weeks before Gettysburg—feared the worst. She contacted Dr. Bourns through a letter written by the town postmaster. Bourns sent a copy of the picture, and when it arrived, Philinda Humiston realized that her husband Amos was dead.

The *American Presbyterian* announced the news on Thursday, November 19, 1863, the same day that President Lincoln delivered the Gettysburg Address.

On January 2, 1864, Dr. Bourns paid a visit to the Humiston home, where he returned the bloodstained ambrotype to Philinda and gave her the profits from the sales of copies of it. He also raised with her the idea of a fundraising drive to establish an orphans' home in Gettysburg for the children of soldiers killed in the war.

Donations poured in from all over the nation, and the orphanage, called the Homestead Orphanage, became a reality in October 1866. With her children, Mrs. Humiston moved to the Homestead, where she was given the job of supervising the children's wardrobe. Three years later, Philinda, unhappy in Gettysburg, married Asa Barnes (a man she met as he passed through town) and moved with him to Massachusetts.

The Homestead Orphanage prospered for several years but met a tragic end, closing after 12 years. The woman who ran the orphanage, Rosa Carmichael, was accused of abusing the children and shackling some of them in the basement. She was convicted of aggravated assault on one of the children. Even Dr. Bourns himself was accused of embezzling large amounts of money from orphanage accounts.

Amos Humiston was born in Owego, New York, in Tioga County on April 26, 1830. After attending a local school, he became a harness maker and then a whaler based in New Bedford, Massachusetts. He responded to President Lincoln's call for 300,000 volunteers in July 1862, enlisting on July 26. He was assigned to the 154th New York and sent to Virginia. On January 25, 1863, he was promoted to sergeant. In March, he required hospitalization for chronic diarrhea or, as he called it, "the Virginia quick step." He recovered and went on to fight at the Wilderness, and later survived a terrible defeat at Chancellorsville on May 2, where the 154th lost 40 percent of its men. Humiston was wounded during the battle and wrote to his wife about missing home. She responded by sending him the ambrotype of their children.

On July 1, 1863, the 154th arrived at Gettysburg and soon were sent into battle. Most of the 154th were captured, but a few Union troops—including Humiston—made a mad dash for safety. He ran less than a quarter-mile before he met his fate.

Amos Humiston is buried in the New York Section of the Gettysburg National Cemetery. In 1999, a biography entitled *Gettysburg's Unknown Soldier: The Life, Death, and Celebrity of Amos Humiston* was published.

Close-up of the monument to Humiston and his children in Gettysburg.

It was written by historian Mark Dunkelman, using Humiston's various war letters.

If You Go:

The monument to Amos Humiston is not in the National Cemetery but instead in the town itself (beside the Gettysburg fire station, on Stratton Street between York Street and the railroad).

See Chapter 4 (John L. Burns) and Chapter 13 (Ginnie Wade) for more information and suggestions if you visit Gettysburg.

6.

JOHN WHITE GEARY

An American Success Story Few Have Heard

County: Dauphin • Town: Harrisburg
Buried at Harrisburg Cemetery
521 North 13th Street

John Geary has a county in Kansas named for him. Kansas also has a Geary State Park. There is a Geary Boulevard in San Francisco, California, named in his honor. There is a Geary Street in both New Cumberland (where he owned a home) and Harrisburg, Pennsylvania. Not to be left out, there is a Geary Street in South Philadelphia as well. There is a monument honoring Geary in Mount Pleasant, Pennsylvania. There is a dorm building at the Pennsylvania State University named Geary Hall. Finally, on August 11, 2007, a statue was unveiled on Culp's Hill, which is part of the Gettysburg Battlefield. It was erected to honor Geary. The subject of this chapter was a man who got around.

Geary was born on December 30, 1819, in what is today the greater Pittsburgh metropolitan area. His father, Richard Geary, was considered a well-educated man. Richard took on the task of educating his two sons. After being prepared by his father, Geary became a student of law and engineering at Jefferson College in Canonsburg, Pennsylvania. Before his graduation, his father passed away, and he was forced to leave school. He found work in Kentucky as a surveyor. While in Kentucky, he also tried his hand at land speculation. He was successful enough to earn the money he needed to return to college, and he graduated in 1841. Upon graduation, he worked at several professions, including mercantile trade and civil engineering. He also studied law and was admitted to the state bar.

John White Geary (by Mathew Brady)

In 1843, Geary married Margaret Ann Logan. In 1846, his first son, Edward, was born. During this time, Geary was employed by the Allegheny Portage Rail Railroad as an engineer. He was instrumental in creating the rail line that traversed the Allegheny Mountains. His ideas would later be used in the construction of the famed Horseshoe Curve.

Geary was already a high ranking officer in the Pennsylvania militia when the Mexican War began in 1846. He formed a company he called the "American Highlanders," all volunteers and all from Cambria County.

This unit was joined with a company from Pittsburgh, and Geary was elected second in command.

The combined unit sailed for Mexico but encountered delays due to both weather and disease. As they approached the Gulf of Mexico, a few cases of smallpox appeared, and the ship was sent to be quarantined. Finally, all signs of the disease disappeared, and on April 12, 1847, Geary and the rest of the company arrived in Vera Cruz. By this time, that city had already been taken by the Americans, so he had to wait for the Battle at Chapultepec to lead his men into an actual engagement with the enemy. He performed heroically and was wounded multiple times during the battle. Considering that he stood at six feet six inches tall and weighed 260 pounds, he must have made for an inviting target. At the war's conclusion, Geary had earned the rank of colonel and returned to the United States a hero of the Mexican War.

After the war, President Polk appointed Geary postmaster of San Francisco. Geary embarked for the west coast with his three-year-old son, his pregnant wife, and thousands of pieces of mail. He and his family arrived in 1849 at the height of the Gold Rush. He quickly dove into his duties, establishing post offices, mail routes, and appointing postmasters. His management skills earned him the admiration of the local citizens. Despite his success in this office, President Taylor, who succeeded Polk, replaced Geary as the postmaster.

It appears that the people of San Francisco did not agree with the new president. In 1850, Geary was easily elected the first mayor of the city. He remains the youngest mayor in San Francisco's history. By this time, due to his wife's failing health, Geary had sent her and his two sons back to Pennsylvania. He remained in California, where he governed capably. He worked hard to get the city's finances in order and was successful. At the same time, he added to his fortune by selling city lots he acquired at little cost to him. In 1852, he returned to Pennsylvania to be with his family and care for his wife. It was to no avail as she passed away in 1853. Geary would remarry in 1858.

At this point in his life, Geary was determined to devote himself to farming and his various business pursuits. This was not to be. His reputation as a war hero and capable administrator led to President Pierce offering him the governorship of the Kansas territory in 1856. At the time, "Bleeding Kansas," as it was called, was a battleground between pro and anti-slavery forces. Geary was not eager to accept the position but acquiesced when Pierce appealed to his patriotic spirit.

In this instance, Geary's initial reluctance may have been correct. His predecessor as governor remarked, "that to govern Kansas in 1855 and 1856, you might as well have attempted to govern the devil in hell." Bleak were the conditions Geary inherited when he arrived in Kansas on September 9, 1856. The Kansas territory was practically a war zone over the issue of slavery. The new governor pledged to be impartial and fair in dealing with the opposition factions in the territory. This policy resulted in the further alienation of both sides.

Geary's problems in Kansas were complicated by the fact that many of President Pierce's appointees in the territory were solidly pro-slavery. These officials resisted Geary's efforts to enforce the law, and bring peace to Kansas. Geary wrote to the president requesting the removal of multiple judges, and the replacement of the federal marshall, the secretary of state, and the attorney general. With a presidential campaign in progress, Pierce determined that the best course was to let his successor handle the problem. James Buchanan of Pennsylvania, who had no record on the issues in Kansas, won the election. Geary lacked confidence in the new president, and he tendered his resignation on March 4, 1857. It was the very day Buchanan was inaugurated. Later in recalling his Kansas experience, Geary wrote, "I have learned more about the depravity of my fellow man than I ever knew before."

After his time in Kansas, Geary returned to Pennsylvania, where he met Mary Church Henderson of Carlisle. Soon, the two were married. In a short time, they welcomed their first child, a girl, whom they named Mary.

Although Geary was a staunch Democrat, he was also firmly anti-slavery. As soon as Geary received word that rebel forces had fired on Fort Sumter, he began recruiting troops. He set up recruiting stations in Philadelphia and elsewhere. Based on his reputation, he had

Geary's monument stands where he fought, atop Culp's Hill on the Gettysburg Battlefield.

little trouble securing volunteers. Sixty-six companies from all over the Commonwealth requested to be put under his command. In the end, Geary formed a 15-company regiment. He and his men saw their first action in October 1861, near Harpers Ferry. In 1862, he led his men across the Potomac and captured the rebel town of Leesburg, Virginia. As a result, Geary was promoted to brigadier general.

Later that year, Geary faced rebel forces under the command of Stonewall Jackson during the Battle of Cedar Mountain. Geary was wounded in both the arm and the leg during the fighting. The wound to the arm was so severe that amputation was considered. While amputation was avoided, Geary was forced to return home to rest and recover.

When Geary returned to the army, he was put in command of the Second Division of the Twelfth Corps under General Slocum. Geary would remain in charge of this division until the war's end. Geary's men saw plenty of action performing heroically at both Chancellorsville and Gettysburg. It was at Gettysburg atop Culp's Hill that Geary and his men repulsed repeated Confederate assaults and succeeded in holding the union's right flank. The action on Culp's Hill cemented Geary's reputation as a Civil War hero. However, the man was not one to rest on his laurels.

In September of 1863, Geary's division was sent to Tennessee to join the forces of Generals Grant and Sherman. On October 27, 1863, Geary's forces were attacked by a superior force of Confederates. In an intense battle known as the Battle of Wauhatchie, the union forces turned back repeated Confederate assaults. During the fighting, Geary's son Eddie was mortally wounded. He died in his father's arms, but Geary and his men held their ground.

Geary's division went on to fight in the Battle of Lookout Mountain, the Atlanta campaign, and Sherman's March to the Sea. He led the Union forces into Savannah, where he was appointed military governor of the city. He ended his army career by serving on the military tribunal that tried Major Henry Wirtz, who had served as commandant of the Andersonville prisoner of war camp. Wirtz was found guilty of war crimes and was hanged in December of 1865.

Geary now returned to Pennsylvania. Though he had always been a Democrat, powerful elements of the Republican Party began looking at him as a potential candidate for governor. Supported by the former Secretary of War, Simon Cameron, Geary was selected to head the Republican ticket in Pennsylvania. He won the election by 17,000 votes and was inaugurated governor in Harrisburg on January 15, 1867.

Geary's grave in the Harrisburg Cemetery is the only one topped by a statue. The monument was erected by the Commonwealth of Pennsylvania.

Geary served two successful terms as governor. He championed education and was a big supporter of Penn State University. He also worked against the influence of the railroads, and for improvements in mine safety. His policies resulted in reduced public debt and an increase in revenues. He left the state in a far better condition than he had found it when he left the governor's office in 1873.

No sooner than Geary left office, rumors began to circulate that he was considering a run for president. That was not to be. Less than three weeks after leaving the office of governor, on February 8, 1873, Geary suffered a massive heart attack and died while preparing breakfast at his home. He was 54 years old.

Geary was given a state funeral that included speeches from the political leaders of the Commonwealth. A large procession followed the funeral to Harrisburg Cemetery where he was laid to rest. His grave is marked by a monument that is topped by a statue of the great man. It is the only statue in the cemetery and was erected by the Commonwealth of Pennsylvania.

If You Go:

See the *"If You Go"* section in *Keystone Tombstones Civil War* Chapter 2 on Simon Cameron.

7.

THOMAS L. KANE

Liberty to the Downtrodden

County: McKean • Town: Kane
Buried at Kane Memorial Chapel
30 Chestnut Street

Thomas Leiper Kane was a Civil War Union brigadier general noted for being the commander of the Pennsylvania Bucktails, perhaps Pennsylvania's most famous Civil War unit. He received a brevet promotion to major general for gallantry at the Battle of Gettysburg.

Kane was born in Philadelphia on January 27, 1822, the son of a prominent Philadelphia judge. After completing college in Philadelphia in 1840, he studied in England for a time and then returned to the U.S. and studied law under his father's direction. He was admitted to the bar in 1846. It was also in that year that Kane became acquainted with the Mormon cause at a conference in Philadelphia. Kane was an abolitionist, as were most Mormons. He offered them his help in their conflicts with the U.S. government and their efforts to emigrate to western territories. He used his father's connections to help the Mormons in Washington, D.C., and influenced the government to enlist a battalion of 500 Mormon men to serve in the campaign against Mexico. While traveling on Mormon business in the summer of 1846, Kane became seriously ill with pulmonary tuberculosis in Fort Leavenworth, Kansas. The members of the church nursed him back to health. During his long convalescence, he decided to devote his life to helping the Mormons and other downtrodden people.

His most significant service was during what became known as the Utah War in the winter of 1857–58. President Buchanan—responding to

Thomas L. Kane

reports that the Mormons were in rebellion—ordered 2,500 U.S. troops to Utah to ensure the installation of Buchanan's appointment of Alfred Cumming (see *Keystone Tombstones Civil War* Chapter 19, "If You Go") as territorial governor, replacing Brigham Young. The Mormons—fearing a forced removal from Utah—were prepared to fight. Kane acted as a mediator and helped arrange a solution that avoided violence.

When the Civil War broke out, Kane had spent two years exploring the Pennsylvania frontier in northwestern Pennsylvania. He immediately offered his services to the Union and was commissioned by Governor Curtin to recruit a regiment of riflemen from the highlands in western Pennsylvania. He recruited woodsmen and lumbermen who were experienced in the woods, could forage for themselves, and could shoot rifles. The latter marksman test for joining the unit was unique, as most volunteers did not have proficiency with a weapon.

This regiment adopted the deer tail as their symbol and became known as the Bucktails, eventually becoming one of the most distinguished units in the Union Army. After the men were trained and equipped, they built rafts so they could float down the west branch of the Susquehanna River to Harrisburg. They reported there, 315 strong, in May 1861 and were officially designated the 42nd Pennsylvania Volunteer Infantry (also referred to as the 13th Pennsylvania Reserves). Although elected colonel by his men, Kane—recognizing his lack of military skill—deferred to a more competent leader and instead became a lieutenant colonel. Veteran Charles J. Biddle was named as the colonel.

Kane was wounded at the Battle of Dranesville, Virginia, on December 20, 1861. It was a painful wound, inflicted by a rifle ball that struck him in the face, knocking out some teeth and crushing the roof of his mouth. For the rest of his life, he wore a full beard to cover the scar.

Soon Biddle resigned to take a seat in Congress, and Kane took over as colonel. He suffered additional wounds while his regiment was fighting Stonewall Jackson's forces in the Shenandoah Valley. At Harrisonburg, Virginia, he was struck by a bullet that split the bone below his knee and, while lying on the ground, he received a brutal crushing blow in the chest from a rifle butt, breaking several ribs. Kane was captured along with Captain Charles Taylor, who refused to leave Kane on the battlefield. He and Taylor were exchanged for Confederate prisoners and returned to duty. Kane's wound would repeatedly reopen for the next two years. Captain Taylor was later killed while fighting by his side at Gettysburg.

Kane participated in the Battle of Catlett's Station and the Second Battle of Bull Run, after which he was promoted to the rank of brigadier general. He led his troops in the Battles of South Mountain, Antietam, Fredericksburg, and Chancellorsville (where he distinguished himself

Gallant attack by 150 of the Pennsylvania Bucktails, led by Colonel Kane, upon a portion of General Stonewall Jackson's Confederate Army, strongly posted in the woods, near Harrisonburg, June 6th, 1862.

despite a Union defeat). After the latter battle, he developed pneumonia and was sent to a hospital in Baltimore, where he would remain until June 1863.

Upon hearing of Lee's invasion of the North, Kane rose from his sickbed to join his men. He traveled by railroad and buggy, at one point, avoiding capture by General J.E.B. Stuart's cavalry by disguising himself as a civilian. He arrived at Gettysburg on the morning of July 2, 1863, and resumed command of his brigade, occupying a position on Culp's Hill. On July 3, the Confederates attacked his position and were repulsed, although Kane fell ill during the fighting and sought assistance from Colonel George Cobham. Despite his brigade's victory, Kane was a broken man and never regained full health. The leg wound left him lame for life, the rifle ball through his cheek and mouth left him tormented by neuralgia, headaches, and poor eyesight, and his weakened lungs made him subject to recurrent respiratory illnesses. He resigned from the Army in November 1863. He bade a sad farewell to his beloved Bucktails and, at the age of 41, limped home to his wife and three children in Philadelphia. At the end of the war, he was breveted to major general.

Kane remained a friend and supporter of the Mormons. In 1872, he and his wife spent the winter in Utah as guests of Brigham Young. When Young died in 1877, Kane returned to Utah to express his sorrow. Kane died in Philadelphia on December 26, 1883, and at first, was buried in Laurel Hill Cemetery in the Kane vault that contains his brother's remains. A year later, the general's remains were moved to a memorial chapel erected in the town named for him. Today the chapel is administered by the Mormons and open to the public. A bronze statue of Thomas Kane is displayed in Utah's Capitol identifying him as a "Friend of the Mormons." Kane County, Utah, was named for him. In 2009, a biography written by Matthew Grow was published, entitled *Liberty to the Downtrodden: Thomas L. Kane, Romantic Reformer.*

If You Go:

The borough of Kane is in a very remote area in northwestern Pennsylvania. The Thomas L. Kane Memorial Chapel is a stone/gothic, revival-style chapel built in 1876–1878. It is listed on the National Register of Historic Places. Outside of the church stands a replica of the Kane statue that resides in the Utah state capitol.

8.

STRONG VINCENT

Don't Give an Inch

County: Erie • Town: Erie
Buried at Erie Cemetery
2116 Chestnut Street

Strong Vincent was a hero at the Battle of Gettysburg, where he sealed with his life the spot entrusted to his keeping and on which so much depended. He was born in Waterford, Pennsylvania (near Erie), on June 17, 1837. He attended Trinity College in Hartford, Connecticut, and graduated from Harvard University in 1859. He was practicing law in Erie when the Civil War broke out. He immediately joined the Pennsylvania militia as a first lieutenant, and on September 14, 1861, he was commissioned lieutenant colonel of the 83rd Pennsylvania Infantry. He was promoted to colonel the following June.

Vincent looked like a soldier should look. He was athletic, barrel-chested, and disciplined. He married his wife, Elizabeth, the same day he enlisted. She was a skilled horsewoman and gave Vincent her riding crop to keep with him for luck. In one of his letters to her, he wrote: "If I fall, remember you have given your husband to the most righteous cause that ever widowed a woman."

In 1862, Vincent fought in the Peninsula Campaign and assumed command of the regiment when his regimental commander was killed on June 27 at the Battle of Gaines's Mill. He then developed a severe case of malaria and was hospitalized until the Battle of Fredericksburg in December of that year. It was around this time that Vincent was offered the position of Judge Advocate for the Army of the Potomac. This position would have assured his safety and his success in civilian

Strong Vincent

life after the war. He declined the position, saying he had joined the army to fight.

On May 20, 1863, Vincent assumed command of the 3rd Brigade, 1st Division, V (Fifth Army) Corps, replacing his brigade commander who was killed at the Battle of Chancellorsville. He turned 26 on the march to Gettysburg and had recently learned that his wife was pregnant with their first child.

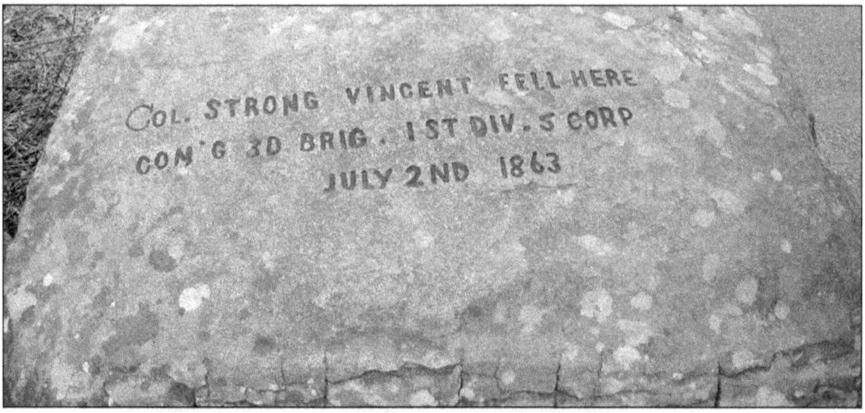

Stone marking where Vincent fell at Gettysburg (photo by Joe Farrell)

At the Battle of Gettysburg, Vincent and his brigade arrived on July 2, the second day of battle. Due to a move against orders, General Daniel Sickles had left a significant terrain feature, Little Round Top, undefended. General Gouverneur K. Warren, the chief engineer of the Army, saw the vital position uncovered and sent for help. He sent couriers scrambling for anyone to occupy and hold the position before the Confederates could. One of the couriers ran into Vincent's brigade and explained the situation. Vincent, without consulting his superior officers, rushed his troops to the hill. His regiments were the 16th Michigan, the 44th New York, the 83rd Pennsylvania, and the 20th Maine, and they were the extreme left flank of the Union line.

The now-famous Colonel Joshua Lawrence Chamberlain led the 20th Maine, and they were the end of the line on the left. Vincent impressed upon Chamberlain the importance of his position ("hold the ground at all hazards"), and then he went to attend to the brigade's right flank. They were attacked within minutes. As the fighting escalated, the 16th Michigan got into trouble and was starting to yield to enemy pressure. Vincent mounted a large boulder and, brandishing his wife's riding crop, cried out to his men, "Don't give an inch!" Moments later, a bullet tore through his thigh and groin and lodged somewhere inside his body. The line held, and Vincent was carried to the Bushman barn nearby. He lingered there for five days and died on July 7, 1863. General George

Stone marker on the Gettysburg battlefield (photo by Joe Farrell)

Meade recommended the promotion to brigadier general, which was approved on July 3, 1863, but it is doubtful that Vincent knew about the honor before he died.

Vincent's wife gave birth to a daughter two months later. Sadly, the baby girl, Blanche, lived only a year. She was buried next to her father in Erie Cemetery. In Gettysburg, there is a monument to Strong Vincent on the south slope of Little Round Top. There is also a carving in a rock marking the spot where he fell nearby. In his hometown of Erie, Strong Vincent High School is named in his honor, and there is a statue of Vincent at Erie's Blasco Library.

One can only speculate on what a future Strong Vincent may have had before him had he survived the war. He was a leader, a bright, educated, handsome, articulate man; and the best and brightest of that time. His country was struggling for its life, and he willingly gave his in that cause.

If You Go:

Also buried in Erie Cemetery is Civil War Medal of Honor recipient William Young (see *Keystone Tombstones Civil War* Chapter 35), and two Civil War Union brevet brigadier generals: Hiram Loomis Brown, who commanded the 145th Pennsylvania Infantry and was wounded at the Battle of Gettysburg; and David Berkley McCreary, also of the 145th Pennsylvania, who was captured at the Battle of Chancellorsville and after the war served as Adjutant General of the Pennsylvania National Guard from 1867 to 1870.

9.

SAMUEL W. CRAWFORD

The Surgeon General

County: Philadelphia • Town: Philadelphia
Buried at Laurel Hill Cemetery
3822 Ridge Avenue

> "I must sustain with honor my flag and the reputation of the name I bear." *—Samuel W. Crawford, delivering his lifelong motto while serving at Fort Sumter.*

Samuel Wylie Crawford was one of only two individuals who were present at Fort Sumter, the outbreak of the Civil War, and at Appomattox Court House for the surrender (the other was General Truman Seymour). Born in Fayetteville, Franklin County, Pennsylvania (just across South Mountain from Gettysburg) on November 8, 1829, Crawford pursued medical studies at the University of Pennsylvania, graduating in 1850. He subsequently joined the Army as a surgeon, serving as such until the outbreak of hostilities in Charleston Harbor in 1861. When the Confederates opened fire on Fort Sumter, commencing what would be a long and bloody war, Crawford commanded several of the cannon that returned fire. A month after this action, Crawford changed career paths, abandoning the surgeon role for a commission as a major in the 13th U.S. Infantry.

By April 25, 1862, Crawford was promoted to brigadier general of volunteers but had yet to see much action. On June 26, Crawford was assigned to Major General John Pope's newly constituted Union "Army of Virginia." The first action of the campaign was at Cedar Mountain on August 9, 1862. Crawford's brigade launched a surprise attack upon

Brigadier General Samuel Wylie Crawford

the Confederate left, routing a division that included the Stonewall Brigade. The Confederates counterattacked, however, and Crawford's brigade, which was unsupported by other units, was driven back with 50% casualties.

An interesting meeting occurred the day after Cedar Mountain. During a truce for burying the dead, Crawford met Rebel cavalry chief

J.E.B. Stuart, whom he had known in the Old Army, on the field. Stuart bet Crawford a hat that the Federals would claim Cedar Mountain had been a Union victory. In due time, under a flag of truce, a hat had arrived at the outpost for Stuart and with it a copy of a New York paper that proclaimed a triumph for Pope in that action. That hat shortly gained notoriety when it was captured in a Union cavalry raid that nearly netted Stuart himself at the start of the Second Bull Run Campaign.

The following month, on September 17, 1862, during what is known as the 'bloodiest single-day battle in American history,' Crawford was heavily engaged at the Battle of Antietam. When the commander of the XII Corps, Major General Joseph K. Mansfield, was killed early at Antietam, the next in line—General Alpheus S. Williams—was elevated and assumed temporary command of the corps. Since Williams was Crawford's superior, Crawford was elevated to Williams's former position. His opportunity was short, however, as Crawford was soon shot in the right thigh and bled profusely. He stayed on the field until he was weakened by the loss of blood and was carried off. Due to the nature of his wounds, he convalesced at his father's home for eight months.

In May of 1863, Crawford returned to the Army, following in the footsteps of Generals John F. Reynolds (see Chapter 1) and George G. Meade (see Chapter 2) as the commander of the Pennsylvania Reserves Division. In late June, in response to Lee's invasion of the North, the Pennsylvania Reserves were added to the Army of the Potomac. On July 2, 1863, the second day of the battle, Crawford and his division arrived at Gettysburg, under the command of Major General George Sykes. Crawford was ordered to assist the brigade of Colonel Strong Vincent (see Chapter 8) at Little Round Top but did not arrive in time to see any action.

Meanwhile, General James Longstreet's Confederates had swept through the Devil's Den, driving the Union defenders back to the west of Little Round Top, to an area that became known to the soldiers as "the Valley of Death." Crawford's division swept down the slope of Little Round Top along with the brigades of Colonels William McCandless and David J. Nevin. While McCandless's brigade led the charge, Crawford

Bronze statue of Crawford on the Gettysburg battlefield (photo by Tammi Knorr)

seized the colors of the First Pennsylvania Reserves from a surprised Corporal Bertless Slot. After a brief struggle and with Corporal Slot running alongside his horse grasping his pant leg, Crawford led his division in a charge that cleared the Valley of Death and, in his estimation, saved Little Round Top.

The following is Crawford's report of the action on July 2:

> "The firing in front was heavy and incessant. The enemy, concentrating his forces opposite the left of our line, was throwing them in heavy masses upon our troops and was steadily advancing. Our troops in front, after a determined resistance, unable to withstand the force of the enemy, fell back, and some finally gave way. The plain to my front was covered with fugitives from all divisions, who rushed through my lines and along the road to the rear. Fragments of regiments came back in disorder, and without their arms, and for a moment, all seemed lost. The enemy's skirmishers had reached the foot of the rocky ridge; his columns were following rapidly . . . Not a moment was to be lost. Uncovering our front, I ordered an immediate advance. The command advanced gallantly with loud cheers. Two well-directed volleys were delivered upon the advancing masses of the enemy, when the whole column charged at a run down the slope, driving the enemy back across the space beyond and across the stone wall, for the possession of which there was a short but determined struggle. The enemy retired to the wheat-field and the woods."

Although this was a relatively minor engagement and casualties were light, Crawford spent the remainder of his life basking in the glory of Little Round Top. The next day, the final day of battle, Crawford was again engaged in a heated struggle, this time with the troops from Georgia and Texas:

> "The line was then formed, and, under the immediate direction of Colonel McCandless, dashed across the wheat-field and into the upper end of the woods. The enemy's skirmishers were driven back as he advanced, and the upper end of the woods was now cleared. The command then changed front to rear and charged through the entire length of woods. One

> brigade of the enemy, commanded by Brigadier General Anderson and composed of Georgia troops, was encountered. It had taken position behind a stone wall running through the woods, and which they had made stronger by rails and logs. We fell upon their flank, completely routing them, taking over 200 prisoners, one stand of colors belonging to the Fifteenth Georgia, and many arms. The colors were taken by Sergt. John B. Thompson, Company G, First Rifles. Another brigade, under General Robertson, and composed of Texas troops, which lay concealed beyond the woods and near the foot of the ridge, ran, as reported by the prisoners, without firing a shot. The enemy's force at this point consisted of the division of Major-General Hood and was composed of three brigades, under the rebel Generals Anderson, Robertson, and Benning. They very greatly outnumbered us, but the rapidity of the movement and the gallant dash of my men completely surprised and routed them. They fell back nearly a mile to a second ridge and entrenched themselves. By this charge of McCandless' brigade and the Eleventh Regiment, Colonel Jackson, the whole of the ground lost the previous day, was retaken, together with all of our wounded, who, mingled with those of the rebels, were lying uncared for. The dead of both sides lay in lines in every direction, and the large number of our own men showed how fierce had been the struggle and how faithfully and how persistently they had contested for the field against the superior masses of the enemy. The result of this movement was the recovery of all the ground lost by our troops, one 12-pounder Napoleon gun, and three caissons, and upward of 7,000 stand of arms. Large piles of these arms were found on brush heaps, ready to be burned."

Though Crawford's men only attacked a small contingent of Longstreet's men on July 2, he later claimed that he had "completely surprised and routed" most of Hood's division. A few months after

Gettysburg, Crawford had the nerve to ask George Sykes to confirm claims which overstated Crawford's division's achievements to the detriment of Sykes's old Regular Division. Sykes refused Crawford's request, blisteringly.

Crawford remained in command of his division through the Overland Campaign (May/June 1864) and the Siege of Petersburg and was again wounded at the Weldon Railroad on August 18, 1864. Crawford was present for Robert E. Lee's surrender at Appomattox Court House in April 1865, making him one of the few soldiers to be present at both the beginning and the effective end of the Civil War.

After the war, Crawford was prominent in preserving the Gettysburg Battlefield and, at one point, attempted to raise money to cover the hill with a large memorial building and museum dedicated to his division. This plan was a failure, and Little Round Top remains close to its original condition, although sprinkled with smaller monuments. Crawford also spent considerable effort politicking to get the official records of the war changed to acknowledge his role as the savior of Little Round Top, but he

Crawford's grave (photo by Joe Farrell)

was also unsuccessful in that quest. Frank Wheaton commented wryly on Crawford's selfishness: "Crawford's innate modesty never prevented his appropriating his full share of all that was done by his division and by [Nevins's Sixth Corps brigade] that afternoon at Gettysburg." Crawford's attempts to garner acclaim, not due him, reached a pathetic state when, after the war, he offered former Confederate Maj. Gen. McLaws "a grade in the army" in exchange for a written acknowledgment that the Pennsylvania Reserves had driven back his forces on July 2nd. McLaws declined.

Crawford was a man very full of himself, never shy about taking full credit for his own and others' achievements on the battlefield. He was "a tall, chesty, glowering man, with heavy eyes, a big nose, and bushy whiskers," as one of his comrades remembered him, who "wore habitually a turn-out-the-guard expression." This description did not do justice to his spectacular sideburns, which reached to his shoulders. He was quite showy, mounted on a handsome "blood bay" horse given to him by Major General William S. Rosecrans. Joshua Chamberlain described him with a slightly acid tone as:

> "a conscientious gentleman, having the entrée at all headquarters, somewhat lofty of manner, not of the iron fiber, nor spring of steel, but punctilious in a way, obeying orders in a certain literal fashion that saved him the censure of superiors—a pet of his State, and likewise, we thought, of Meade and Warren, judging from the attention they always gave him—possibly not quite fairly estimated by his colleagues as a military man . . ."

Crawford retired from the Army on February 19, 1873, and was given the rank of brigadier general, U.S. Army Retired. He was the author of *The Genesis of the Civil War*, published in 1887. On November 3, 1892, he died in Philadelphia and was buried there in Laurel Hill Cemetery.

If You Go:

Also buried in Laurel Hill Cemetery are four men who were brevetted brigadier generals in March or April 1865 for "meritorious service." They are:

- **Alexander Cummings:** nicknamed "Old Straw Hat." He served as commander of the 19th Pennsylvania Volunteer Cavalry, and as the Superintendent of Colored Troops in the Department of Arkansas after the Union opted to allow black troops into the army.
- **Robert Thompson:** commanded the 115th Pennsylvania Volunteer Infantry.
- **William Redwood Price:** served in a variety of administrative posts in Washington, D.C.
- **William Delaware Lewis, Jr.:** commanded the 110th Pennsylvania Volunteer Infantry.

10.

SAMUEL K. ZOOK

The Mennonite Master of Profanity

County: Montgomery • Town: Norristown
Buried at Montgomery Cemetery
1 Hartranft Avenue

From his obelisk monument at the Wheatfield on the Gettysburg Battlefield:

To the memory of
Samuel
Kosciusko Zook.
Brevet Major
General U.S. Vols.
Who fell mortally
wounded at or near
this spot. while
gallantly leading
his brigade in battle
July 2nd, 1863.
Erected by Gen. Zook
Post. No 11 G.A.R.
of Norristown, Pa.
July 25th, 1882.

General Samuel Kosciuszko Zook (born Samuel Kurtz Zook) (March 27, 1821–July 3, 1863) was born and raised in Tredyffrin Township, Chester County, Pennsylvania, not far from George Washington's

Samuel K. Zook

Valley Forge encampment. On his father's side, he was descended from Mennonites; specifically, the Anabaptist order started by Menno Simmons in Switzerland. As a boy, Zook played soldier on the earthworks where the Revolutionary War soldiers roamed. His grandfather Zook was a major during the American Revolution. As a young man, he decided to take Kosciuszko as his middle name, in honor of the Revolutionary

War general from Poland who assisted the Americans. Of course, all this martial activity among the Zooks is contrary to the pacifist practices of the Mennonites. The Zooks had not been pacifists for several generations.

In the years before the Civil War, Zook was a pioneer in the information technology of his day—the telegraph. As Kenneth Silverman writes in his book *Lightning Man: The Accursed Life of Samuel B. Morse*:

> "On the New Orleans route, O'Reilly intended to use what he advertised as 'A NEW AND IMPROVED TELEGRAPH (and NOT Morse's plan).' Not Morse's, or House's either. While publicly beating the drum for House's telegraph, he had always privately thought it 'not simple enough.' For his potentially lucrative line to New Orleans, he chose an instrument called the Columbian telegraph, designed by two young telegraphers in his Cincinnati office, Samuel K. Zook and E. F. Barnes. Admirers of the Columbian alleged that it differed from Morse's system in two ways. Its registers used permanent magnets instead of electromagnets; and it had a novel galvanometer-like relay that supposedly protected transmission during thunderstorms. . . ."

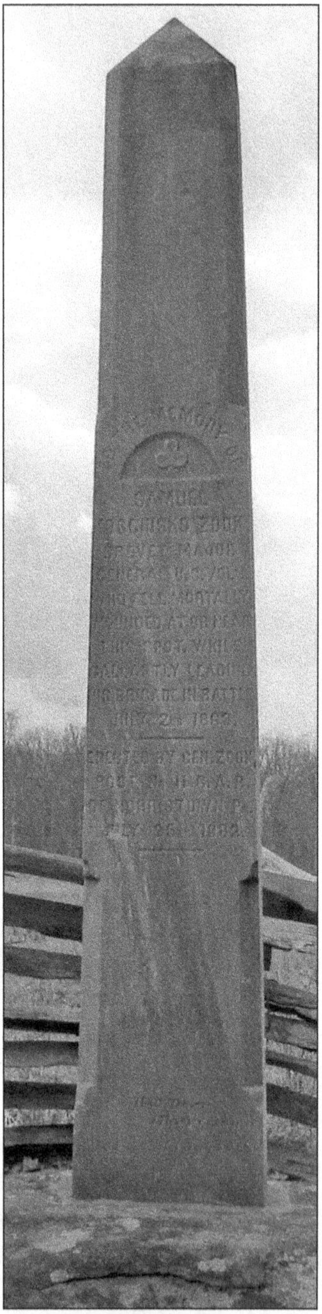
Zook's obelisk

Morse thought this was an infringement of his patent and the two sides battled for years in the marketplace. When the patent suit was heard in September 1848, the judge ruled for Morse. O'Reilly was not deterred and continued his battles for several more years before eventually relenting. Zook, meanwhile, moved to New York City and became the superintendent of the Washington and New York Telegraph Company. While in New York, he had risen to lieutenant colonel in the 6th New York Governor's Guard by the time of the Civil War.

During the summer of 1861, while with the 6th New York Militia, Zook served as the military governor of Annapolis. When this 90-day regiment was mustered out (thanks to connections made in Annapolis), he raised a new regiment—the 57th New York, to which he was the colonel.

Zook's first action was in 1862, serving in Major General Edwin V. Sumner's division of the Army of the Potomac, during the Seven Days Battles. While scouting enemy positions at the Battle of Gaines's Mill, Zook noticed a Confederate deception regarding troop numbers. Zook reported this discovery up to General George McClellan but was ignored, and an opportunity was lost.

Zook missed the Battle of Antietam while on medical leave but returned in time for Fredericksburg. There, he served in the division of Major General Winfield S. Hancock (see Chapter 3). Zook's brigade arrived early at the battle. Zook recognized the Union could gain a significant advantage if he could cross the Rappahannock River immediately. However, the new commander of the Army of the Potomac, Ambrose Burnside, preferred to wait until more troops arrived, and pontoon bridges could be put in place. Wrote Zook of this missed opportunity:

> "If we had had the pontoons promised when we arrived here, we could have the hills on the other side of the river without cost over 50 men—now it will cost at least 10,000 if not more."

While he waited, Zook served as military governor of Falmouth, Virginia. During the ensuing battle, Zook's brigade led the first assault on Marye's Heights, achieving one of the farthest advances of the battle.

Zook had his horse shot out from under him as the Confederates repulsed the attack. Hancock was incredibly pleased with Zook's bravery on the field. In March 1863, Zook was promoted to brigadier general. Zook wrote about the Fredericksburg battle:

> "I walked over the field, close under the enemy's picket line, last night about 3 o'clock. The ground was strewn thickly with corpses of the heroes who perished there on Saturday. I never realized before what war was. I never before felt so horribly since I was born. To see men dashed to pieces by shot & torn into shreds by shells during the heat and crash of battle is bad enough, God knows, but to walk alone amongst slaughtered brave in the 'still small hours' of the night would make the bravest man living 'blue.' God grant, I may never have to repeat my last night's experience." —*Samuel K. Zook, letter to E. I. Wade, December 16, 1862*

Zook had a reputation for being a disciplinarian and a master of profanity, despite his Mennonite background. While on the road to Chancellorsville, he was one half of a famous battle of profanity with General Hancock. Wrote an enlisted man about the incident: "It was the greatest cursing match I ever listened to; Zook took advantage of Hancock, by waiting until the latter got out of breath, and then he opened his pipe organ, and the air was very blue."

Zook fought at Chancellorsville and then missed some time due to rheumatism. He returned to the field in time for Gettysburg, where he served under Brigadier General John C. Caldwell. On the second day, at the Wheatfield, while reinforcing Stony Hill, which was under attack by Longstreet, Zook was shot three times in the shoulder, chest, and abdomen. He was moved to the Hoke house on the Baltimore Pike, in the care of Dr. William Potter, a friend of the general. Wrote Potter about Zook's wounds: "fatally shot, a shell having torn open his left shoulder and chest, exposing the heart-beats to observation."

Zook's grave

Zook succumbed to his wounds the next day. He was posthumously awarded the rank of major general. Samuel K. Zook is buried near his good friend and cursing partner General Winfield S. Hancock, at Montgomery Cemetery, near Norristown, Pennsylvania.

If You Go:

See the *"If You Go"* sections of Chapter 3 (Winfield Hancock) and *Keystone Tombstones Civil War* Chapter 8 (John Hartranft).

II.

GETTYSBURG GENERALS

This chapter will feature several generals who fought at the monumental Battle of Gettysburg: David Bell Birney; Alexander Hays; Thomas Rowley; David McMurtrie Gregg; and Alexander Schimmelfennig.

David Bell Birney

County: Philadelphia • Town: Philadelphia
Buried at Woodlands Cemetery
4000 Woodlands Cemetery

David Bell Birney was a controversial figure. He was the son of James B. Birney, a Kentuckian who had once owned slaves but later became one of the country's most vehement abolitionists. Birney's father had an international reputation; he ran twice for President (1840 and 1844) and published a weekly abolitionist publication while living in Cincinnati, Ohio.

General Birney

When the Civil War broke out, Birney was practicing law in Philadelphia very successfully and had many influential clients and friends. The family had moved to Philadelphia because of numerous threats from pro-slavery mobs. Birney foresaw the coming of the war; in 1860, he began studying military science and got appointed as a lieutenant colonel of the Pennsylvania militia. When the war began, he was appointed to colonel in August 1861, and then to brigadier general in February 1862. These were purely political promotions, however, and they spawned a lot of envy and resentment. At the Battle of Seven Pines, Virginia, on May 31, 1862, he was removed from command and accused of disobeying an order from corps command. He was court-martialed but acquitted and restored to command.

Birney's grave

Birney fought at the Second Battle of Bull Run, losing over 600 men in intense fighting. While fighting at Fredericksburg, he again encountered military discipline problems for balking at an order—yet once again, he was ultimately able to escape punishment. He went on to lead his brigades in extremely heavy fighting at Chancellorsville, suffering still more heavy casualties. After Chancellorsville, he was promoted to major general.

On the second day of the Battle of Gettysburg, Birney was part of General Daniel Sickles's insubordinate and foolish abandonment of their assigned defensive position on Cemetery Ridge and subsequent movement to Devil's Den, the Wheatfield, and the Peach Orchard. They were attacked and decimated by Confederate troops under the command of Generals Hood and McLaws. Birney himself received two minor wounds. The entire III (Third Army) Corps was finished as a fighting force.

He emerged months later as division commander in II (Second Army) Corps and served well in the Wilderness, Spotsylvania Court House (where he was again wounded), and Cold Harbor. In July 1864, General Grant gave Birney command of X (Tenth Army) Corps in the Army of the James. During the Siege of Petersburg, he fell ill with typhoid fever.

He returned to Philadelphia, where he died on October 18, 1864. He is buried in Woodlands Cemetery.

If You Go:

Woodlands Cemetery is itself a National Historic Landmark and has many interesting graves and noteworthy people buried there. There are several other Civil War generals buried there. Among them are:

- **Brevet Brigadier General Hartman Bache**, who was a great-grandson of Benjamin Franklin and brother-in-law of General George Meade.
- **Brevet Major General James Gwyn**, who distinguished himself in the Battle of Poplar Spring Church and the Battle of Five Forks.
- **Brevet Brigadier General Charles Herring**, who lost his right leg at the Battle of Dabney's Mills, Virginia, and gained distinction at the Battle of Hatcher's Run, Virginia.
- **Brevet Brigadier General James Lynch**, who was cited for his action at the Battle of Deep Bottom, Virginia.
- **Brevet Brigadier General John Abercrombie**, who was wounded at the Battle of Fair Oaks, Virginia, and was one of the oldest officers to serve on the battlefield.
- **Brevet Major General George Crosman**, who served as Chief Quartermaster of the Philadelphia Depot.
- **Brevet Major General John Ely**, who served as commander of the 23rd Pennsylvania Volunteer Infantry.
- **Brevet Brigadier General Clement Finley**, who served as Surgeon General of the Army when the war broke out (retiring in 1862).
- **Brevet Brigadier General John Quincy Lane**, who served as colonel and commander of the 97th Ohio Volunteer Infantry.
- **Brevet Brigadier General Richard Price**, who as commander of the 2nd Pennsylvania Volunteer Cavalry, gained distinction by capturing the colonel of the 6th Virginia Cavalry in September 1862.

Also buried at Woodlands Cemetery are two Civil War Medal of Honor recipients: Sylvester Bonnaffon, Jr., and Thomas Cripps. Bonnaffon was awarded the Medal of Honor for his service at the Battle of Boydton Plank

Road, Virginia, where he was severely wounded. Cripps was awarded the Medal of Honor for bravery during the Union naval assault on Mobile Bay, Alabama, on August 5, 1864.

There is also a large, prominent grave in Woodlands for Henry Boyd McKeen, who served as colonel of the 81st Pennsylvania Volunteer Infantry. He was wounded at Chancellorsville and led his regiment in the Wheatfield and Rose Woods on the second day at Gettysburg, as well as the battles of the Wilderness and Spotsylvania. He was killed at the Battle of Cold Harbor.

Woodlands is also the final resting place for Civil War figures Dr. Jacob Mendez Da Costa and Emily Bliss Souder. Dr. Da Costa was the first to identify what has become known as "post-traumatic stress disorder" while serving as an assistant surgeon in the Union Army. He called it "irritable heart" or "soldier's heart," and later, it became known as Da Costa syndrome. Souder was a volunteer nurse at the Battle of Gettysburg and author of *Leaves from the Battlefield of Gettysburg*, published in 1864.

Alexander Hays

County: Allegheny • Town: Pittsburgh (Lawrenceville)
Buried at Allegheny Cemetery
4734 Butler Street

Alexander Hays was born in Franklin, Pennsylvania, on July 8, 1819. He attended Allegheny College and then transferred to the United States Military Academy, where he became a close friend of Ulysses S. Grant. He served in the Mexican American War then returned to civilian life and was a civil engineer for the city of Pittsburgh when the Civil War broke out. He re-entered the service as colonel of the 63rd Pennsylvania Infantry. He led his troops in battles at Yorktown, Williamsburg, Seven Pines, Savage's Station, and Malvern Hill, after which he suffered blindness in his right eye and partial paralysis of his left arm.

He returned to duty in time for the Second Battle of Bull Run, where he led a charge and received a painful wound that shattered his leg and put him out of action for many months.

Hays was a fiery, emotional fighter and had an extraordinary intensity when he returned to command at Gettysburg. His division defended the right of the Union line on Cemetery Ridge. They held firm in the repulse of the Confederate attack on July 3, even counterattacking the left flank of the Confederate force. When the smoke cleared, Hays was unhurt but had had two horses shot from under him. In his exhilaration, he grabbed a Rebel battle flag and rode down his division's line dragging it in the dirt behind his horse. After the battle, Hays explained:

> "I was fighting for my native state, and before I went [in] I thought of those at home I so dearly love. If Gettysburg was lost all was lost for them, and I only interposed a life that would be otherwise worthless."

Hays went on to lead a division at the Battle of Morton's Ford, where there were stories of him being drunk during battle.

Bronze statue of General Hays at Gettysburg (Photo by Tammi Knorr)

Grave of General Hays

On the first day of the Battle of the Wilderness, May 5, 1864 (during the earliest phase of the Overland Campaign), Hays was killed when a Confederate bullet struck him in the head.

Hays was buried in Allegheny Cemetery in Pittsburgh. Ulysses S. Grant visited Hays's grave during a campaign stop in his run for the presidency. Grant wept openly for his friend. A statue of General Hays stands on the Gettysburg Battlefield (at Cemetery Ridge), and a monument marks the spot where he was killed in the Wilderness.

If You Go:

Allegheny Cemetery is a large, historical treasure with many interesting graves. Thomas Rowley is buried there (see below), as are Medal of Honor Recipients Archibald Rowand and Major General Alfred Pearson.

Also of interest are the graves of Brigadier General Conrad Jackson, who was killed at the Battle of Fredericksburg, and Brigadier General James Scott Negley, who commanded Union forces at the Battle of Chattanooga and was relieved of his command after the defeat at Chickamauga.

Thomas Rowley

County: Allegheny • Town: Pittsburgh (Lawrenceville)
Buried at Allegheny Cemetery
4734 Butler Street

Thomas Algeo Rowley was born in Pittsburgh on October 5, 1808. He entered the United States military service in the Mexican War as a captain of a company of volunteers in 1847. He served with this company until July 1848, when he was honorably mustered out and returned to peaceful pursuits as a cabinet maker.

At the start of the Civil War, Rowley was a clerk of the courts for Allegheny County when commissioned a major in the 13th Pennsylvania Volunteers. After a few months, the army was reorganized, and he was promoted to colonel of the 102nd Pennsylvania Infantry. He led forces in

General Rowley

General Rowley's grave

the Peninsula Campaign at Yorktown, Williamsburg, Fair Oaks (where he was wounded), and Malvern Hill. He distinguished himself at the Battle of Fredericksburg and was promoted to brigadier general on November 29, 1862. He next commanded a brigade at the Battle of Chancellorsville.

The day before the Battle of Gettysburg, Rowley was given command of a division due to the death of General John Reynolds (see Chapter 1). What happened on July 1, 1863, the first day of the battle, is mired in controversy. The I (First) Army Corps line gave way under the Confederate onslaught led by General Harry Heth. The Union troops retreated through the streets of Gettysburg to the heights of Cemetery Hill. During this retreat, Rowley—who suffered from severe boils that made it difficult for him to remain on his mount—fell from his horse. Soon after that, he had a confrontation with Brigadier General Lysander Cutler, who concluded from Rowley's actions and demeanor that he was drunk. Rowley was placed under arrest for drunkenness and disobedience. A court-martial subsequently convicted him.

The testimony was conflicting. Rowley's inexperience, distracting, and painful physical ailment, and the blistering heat may have led to his strange behavior. His alleged drunkenness was never proven to the satisfaction of Secretary of War Edwin Stanton, who reinstated him. When assigned only a district command and not a field command, Rowley resigned in December 1864.

After the war, Rowley served as a U.S. marshal and practiced law. He died on May 14, 1892, and is buried in Allegheny Cemetery. A book entitled *Disgrace at Gettysburg: The Arrest and Court Martial of Brigadier General Thomas A. Rowley*, was written by John F. Krumwiede and published in 2006.

David McMurtrie Gregg

County: Berks • Town: Reading
Buried at Charles Evans Cemetery
1119 Centre Avenue

David McMurtrie Gregg was born in Huntingdon, Pennsylvania, on April 10, 1833. He was the first cousin of future Pennsylvania Governor Andrew Curtin (see *Keystone Tombstones Civil War* Chapter 3). He graduated from the United States Military Academy in 1855. While a cadet, he came to know J.E.B. Stuart, who was a year ahead of him. His first assignment was in the New Mexico Territory as a company commander in the 1st U.S. Dragoons. When Fort Sumter was attacked, Gregg was called to Washington and assigned to the cavalry. In October 1861, he was stricken with a severe case of typhoid fever and was hospitalized in Washington. While there, he barely escaped death when the hospital caught fire. When he recovered, he became the colonel of the 8th Pennsylvania Cavalry. The 8th Pennsylvania took part in the

Equestrian statue of General Gregg at Centre Avenue in Reading, Pennsylvania (photo by Lawrence Knorr)

Peninsula Campaign, particularly in the Seven Days Battle, where they served as a screen between the Confederates and the retreating Union Army. He was at Antietam, but cavalry played a minor role.

While on furlough on October 6, 1862, Gregg married Ellen Sheaff at St. Thomas Church in Whitemarsh, Pennsylvania. After honeymooning in New York City, he was promoted to brigadier general and sent to participate in the Battle of Fredericksburg, where again, the cavalry was held in reserve and underutilized. At Chancellorsville, the Cavalry Corps (including Gregg's 3rd Division) were ineffective, and General Alfred Pleasonton was put in charge of the Cavalry Corps replacing General George Stoneman.

In early June, the Federal Cavalry was again reorganized, and Gregg was made commander of the 2nd Division. As the Confederate troops moved north into Pennsylvania, his division engaged them at Aldie (June 17), Middleburg (June 18-19), and Upperville (June 21). Gregg's division arrived in Gettysburg mid-day on July 2 and took up positions to protect the right flank of the Union Army. On July 3, Gregg's division, along with General Custer's brigade, met J.E.B. Stuart's cavalry in what is now called "East Cavalry Field." A lengthy mounted battle—including hand-to-hand combat—ensued. Stuart was blocked from achieving his goals.

Gregg led his cavalry division in almost two years of hard fighting after Gettysburg, including the Battle of Yellow Tavern, where J.E.B. Stuart—his friend from West Point—was killed, dealing the Confederacy a severe blow.

Gregg resigned his commission on January 25, 1865, for personal reasons. He missed the end of the war, and his real reasons for quitting are not known. In a biography of General John Buford, the writer (Edward Longacre) claims that Gregg feared a violent death and simply lost his nerve.

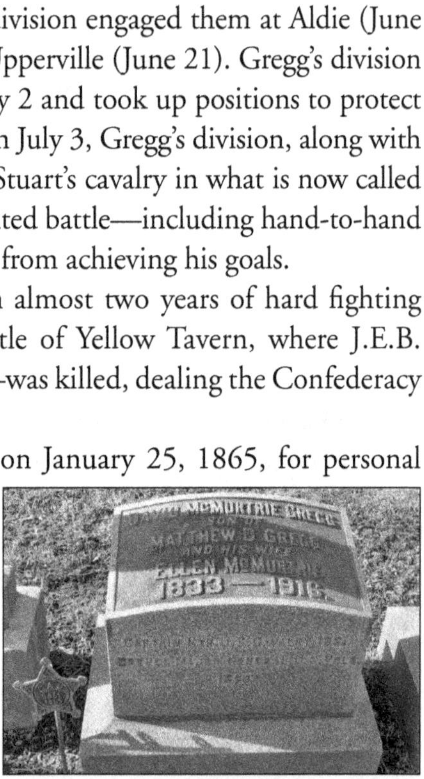

Final resting place of General Gregg

Gregg was reportedly bored with life as a farmer. He became

active in state and local affairs and visited Gettysburg numerous times. In 1891, he was elected to a term as Auditor General of Pennsylvania.

Gregg died in Reading, Pennsylvania, on August 17, 1916, at the age of 83, the last of Pennsylvania's Civil War leaders. He is buried in historical Charles Evans Cemetery and memorialized with a life-sized bronze equestrian statue at North Fourth Street and Centre Avenue in Reading. Buried near Gregg in Charles Evans Cemetery is the prominent grave of Alexander Schimmelfennig (see below).

Alexander Schimmelfennig

County: Berks • Town: Reading
Buried at Charles Evans Cemetery
1119 Centre Avenue

Alexander Schimmelfennig was born in Germany in 1824. A graduate of the German military academy, he took part in the failed 1848 German Revolution. He was wounded twice in battle, captured, rescued, and eventually fled to Switzerland. For his involvement, he was tried in absentia and sentenced to death by the Prussian authorities.

General Schimmelfenning

In 1854 Schimmelfennig emigrated to the United States. At the start of the Civil War, he joined the Union Army and helped organize the 74th Pennsylvania Volunteer Infantry out of mostly German immigrants; he was commissioned its colonel in July 1861. In August 1862, he fought at the Second Battle of Bull Run and was promoted to brigadier general in November. He commanded a division of mostly Germans at the Battle of Chancellorsville in May 1863. The Corps performance at Chancellorsville came under significant criticism in the press and by corps commander General Otis Howard, as they engaged in a mass retreat after being flanked by Stonewall Jackson.

At the subsequent Battle of Gettysburg, Schimmelfennig commanded the 1st Brigade in XI Corps. On the first day of the battle, his men were driven back in a retreat through town, and many were captured. During the retreat, Schimmelfennig briefly hid in a culvert on Baltimore Street. Then—stunned from having his horse shot from under him and cut off by the advancing Confederates—Schimmelfennig successfully avoided capture by hiding out in a shed on the Anna Garlach property for several days (until July 4).

After the battle, Schimmelfennig rejoined the corps, but his story was seized upon by the press and was promulgated as yet another example of German cowardice.

In the fall of 1863, he and his brigade were reassigned to the Carolinas and participated in the Carolinas Campaign. He was in command in Charleston, South Carolina, when the Confederates surrendered on February 18, 1865.

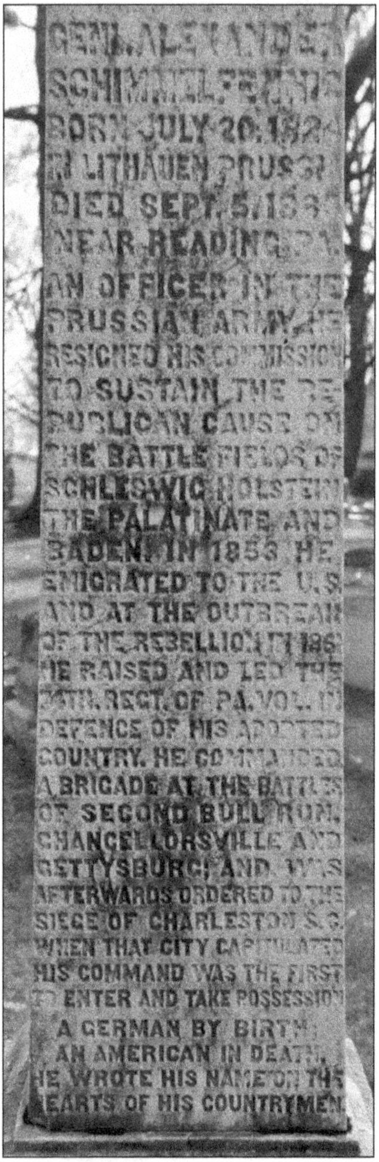

Detail of Schimmelfennig's grave (Photo by Lawrence Knorr)

During his time of service in the swamps around Charleston, he contracted a form of tuberculosis that ultimately led to his death. He died on September 5, 1865, in Wernersville, Pennsylvania, having traveled there to visit a mineral springs sanatorium in the hopes of finding a cure for his disease.

If You Go:

Also, in historic Charles Evans Cemetery is the grave of Brigadier General William High Keim. Keim was a U.S. Congressman and Mayor of Reading before the war. He was commissioned general of the Pennsylvania militia and then brigadier general of volunteers. He participated in the Peninsula Campaign until he died of typhus in Harrisburg on May 18, 1862.

12.

DENNIS O'KANE

The Fighting Irishman

County: Philadelphia • Town: Philadelphia
Buried at Old Cathedral Cemetery
48th Street & Lancaster Avenue

He was born in Derry, Ireland, in 1818. He left Ireland and came to America with a wife and two daughters. After settling in Philadelphia, he and his wife had their third daughter. On July 3, 1863, he found himself on Cemetery Ridge in Gettysburg, commanding the 69th Pennsylvania Volunteers. His name was Dennis O'Kane.

The 69th Pennsylvania was part of the Philadelphia Brigade. It was made up mainly of Irish immigrants or the children of Irish immigrants. The 69th had been involved in numerous battles, including the Second Bull Run, South Mountain, Antietam, Fredericksburg, Chancellorsville, and Gettysburg.

O'Kane almost did not make it to Gettysburg. Nine months earlier, he had faced a court-martial. At the time, the 69th was at Harpers Ferry, and O'Kane's wife and eldest daughter had come to visit him. O'Kane rented a carriage and horses and proceeded to show his wife and daughter around the town. During the trip, O'Kane's commanding officer, Colonel Joshua Owen, showed up drunk and on horseback. He proceeded to guide his mount against the carriage horses. When he repeated the maneuver, O'Kane called out to him to stop it. At that point, Owen called O'Kane an Irish son of a bitch, and then he invited O'Kane's wife to spend the night with him in his tent. O'Kane immediately jumped from the carriage, grabbed Owen, and pulled him from his horse. Owen's head bounced as it hit the ground. This led to O'Kane's court-martial,

Dennis O'Kane

but he was acquitted. It also led to the dismissal of Owen and O'Kane's rise to command the 69th.

O'Kane was present on the third day of the Battle of Gettysburg when the Confederate cannons began the bombardment that would precede Pickett's Charge. During the shelling, O'Kane observed General Hancock calmly riding among the troops who had hit the ground for protection. Hancock, who had presided at O'Kane's court-martial, waved to O'Kane, and O'Kane responded with a salute.

Currier and Ives print of the highwater mark at Gettysburg

When the shelling ended and the smoke lifted, O'Kane could see the Confederates emerging from the woods on Seminary Ridge, making their way towards his troops. O'Kane reminded the men of the 69th that they were fighting today to protect their state. He ordered the 69th's colors uncased, and the green flag with a golden harp on one side and the Pennsylvania coat of arms on the other was soon in the air.

The Union artillery opened on the advancing Confederates, opening holes in their lines that other rebel soldiers rushed to fill as the charge continued. The soldiers of the 69th watched from behind a stone wall as the Confederates drew nearer. When a section of the Union line manned by the 71st Pennsylvania retreated, the 69th was unprotected on its right side. The Confederate General Lewis Armistead, with his hat resting on the tip of his sword, led his men toward that very spot. O'Kane then ordered his men to turn to the right and face the enemy. During the fighting that followed, O'Kane saw General Armistead collapse after being wounded. Shortly after that, O'Kane himself was seriously wounded and had to be removed from the field but not before knowing that his troops had played a crucial part in repulsing the Confederate attack.

O'Kane's grave

O'Kane died the next day, July 4, 1863. His funeral was held in Philadelphia at Saint James Church. His pallbearers were Union Army officers. After mass, his remains were transported to Cathedral Cemetery where he was laid to rest with full military honors.

If You Go:

Civil War Brigadier General Richard Dillon is also buried at Cathedral Cemetery. Dillon lost an arm at the Battle of Chancellorsville. He was brevetted brigadier general on March 13, 1865, for gallant and meritorious service during the war.

Cathedral Cemetery is also the final resting place for Civil War Medal of Honor recipient Edmund English. He received this honor for his actions during the Battle of the Wilderness. His citation reads that "during a rout and under orders to retreat, seized the colors, rallied the men, and drove the enemy back."

Also, Civil War Union Brevet Major General and Medal of Honor recipient St. Clair Augustine Mulholland was laid to rest at Cathedral Cemetery (see *Keystone Tombstones Civil War* Chapter 11).

13.

GINNIE WADE

A Tragic Love Story

County: Adams • Town: Gettysburg
Buried at Evergreen Cemetery
799 Baltimore Street

On June 26, 1863, the Confederate troops first entered Gettysburg, and for a twenty-year-old local girl, it was a scary and frantic day. The Confederates had arrested her brother Samuel Wade for failing to obey orders to hand over the family horse to Confederate troops. Mary Virginia (Ginnie or Jennie) Wade was helping to care for Isaac Brinkerhoff, a six-year-old disabled neighborhood boy, when she heard of her brother's arrest and went to try to secure an arrest release from General Jubal Early.

Mary Wade was born on Baltimore Street in Gettysburg on May 21, 1843. When she grew older, she worked as a seamstress with her mother in their house on Breckenridge Street while her father was in a mental asylum. When Union troops arrived on July 1 and shooting began, Ginnie went to her sister's house on Baltimore Street to assist her sister Georgia McClellan with her newborn baby. She never expected that the McClellan house would be situated between Union and Confederate lines during the three-day battle.

As the fighting wore on, Union troops began asking the family for food and water. Surely Ginnie must have thought of her fiancé Johnston (Jack) Skelly, who was serving as a member of the 87th Pennsylvania Volunteer Infantry. She and Skelly and their friend Wesley Culp had been schoolmates who became close friends and often played together on nearby Culp's Hill. Wesley Culp had moved to Virginia and enlisted with the 2nd Virginia Infantry and was now engaged in a great battle on the

Mary Virginia "Ginnie" or "Jennie" Wade

farm where he was born and raised. Ginnie decided to do what she could for the Union troops and spent her time filling canteens and baking bread. What she didn't know was that her beloved Jack Skelly had been badly wounded and captured by the Confederates at the battle of Carter's Woods near Winchester, Virginia. Wesley Culp also fought in that battle against her friend, a brother William, and a cousin David Culp. Wesley Culp met up with the wounded Skelly after the battle, and Skelly gave him a message for Ginnie Wade should he make it back to Gettysburg someday. Culp did manage to slip away from the fighting to visit his two sisters on the Culp farm but discovered Ginnie had left her home to stay at her sister's and was in the crossfire between the lines. Shortly after, on July 2, Wesley Culp was killed within sight of the house where he had been born. He was never able to deliver his message to Ginnie Wade.

Ginnie had worked hard for two days, but on July 3, 1863, she awoke at 4:30 in the morning to prepare bread for the Union soldiers. Soon after, the house came under Confederate fire. Georgia McClellan later noted the last words Ginnie spoke to her. According to Georgia, Ginnie said, "If there is anyone in this house that is to be killed today, I hope it is me." According to Georgia, Ginnie didn't want any harm to come to her sister because she had a baby.

That day around 8:30 A.M., Ginnie was kneading dough for bread when a bullet came through a wooden door into the kitchen of the house and struck her in the back, killing her instantly. She had a picture of Jack Skelly in her apron pocket. She was buried in her sister's garden the following day, and her mother baked 15 loaves of bread with the dough Ginnie had kneaded.

She never got Jack Skelly's message, nor the news that he died nine days later on July 12 from his wounds. The two passed away without knowing the other's fate.

In January 1864, her body was relocated to the cemetery of the German Reformed Church on Stratton Street and, in November 1865, again relocated to the Evergreen Cemetery close to Jack Skelly.

Wesley Culp's commanding officer sent his orderly to Culp's sister's to notify them where to find his body. Some say he was never found, but his gun with his name carved in the stock was located. Others say that being a Confederate, he was secretly buried in Evergreen Cemetery. Some believe he was buried in the cellar of the Culp Farm House.

Ginnie Wade was the only civilian killed directly during the battle of Gettysburg. An elaborate monument marks her grave, including an American flag that flies around the clock. The only other site devoted to a woman that shares the distinction of the perpetual flag is that of the Betsy Ross House in Philadelphia.

In 1996, a book about Ginnie Wade was published. It was written by Cindy Small and called *The Jennie Wade Story*. You might notice the different spelling of Ms. Wade's name. Although Cindy Small used the "Jennie," and so does the Jennie Wade House in Gettysburg, the research we did says it is unlikely anyone ever called her Jennie. Her middle name was Virginia, and she was known as Ginnie. A newspaper account of her story shortly after the battle used the name "Jennie," and it spread all over the country.

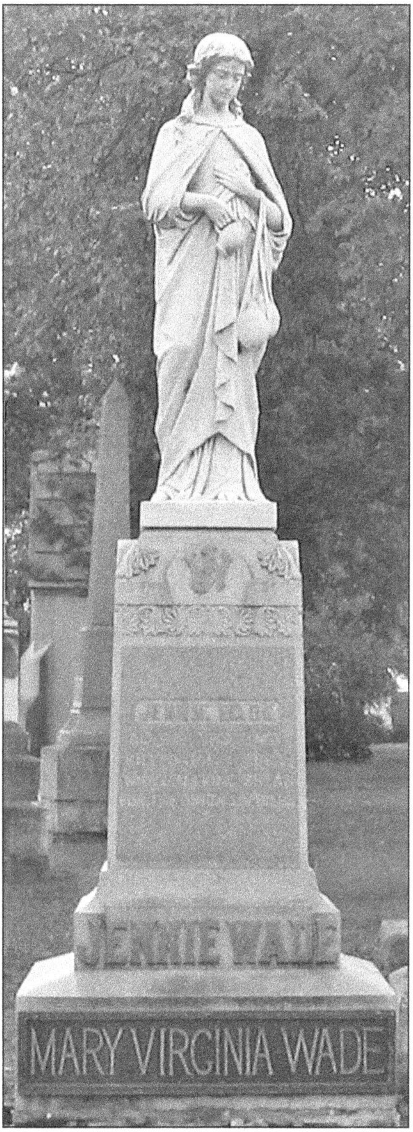

The only civilian killed during the Battle of Gettysburg.

If You Go:

Gettysburg is a history buff's paradise. The Evergreen Cemetery also contains many historic and interesting graves, including John Burns (see Chapter 4) and Major League Baseball Hall of Famer Eddie Plank (see *Keystone Tombstones Volume 2* Chapter 17). Other graves of interest include James Gettys, the founder of Gettysburg, and a soldier in the Pennsylvania Militia during the Revolution. His wife, Mary Todd, was an ancestor of Mary Todd Lincoln.

Elizabeth Thorn was the caretaker of Evergreen Cemetery during the Civil War. Her husband Peter enlisted in the 138th Pennsylvania and left her to care for the cemetery. She averaged five burials a month until the Battle of Gettysburg. At the time, she was six months pregnant, and her duties became overwhelming. A memorial at the gatehouse depicts a pregnant Elizabeth attending her duties.

Stephen Courson, a former Pittsburgh Steeler who played in two Super Bowl Championship games and authored *False Glory* in 1991, was also laid to rest here. The book tells of steroid use in the NFL.

Jennie Wade's fiancé who died fighting for the Union.

Also in Gettysburg is the famous Battlefield, the National Cemetery (we mention some interesting graves there in the chapter on John Burns), the Eisenhower Farm, and the Jennie Wade house, among other historical sites. The Jennie Wade House is the site of her tragic death on Baltimore Street. The House is marked by over 150 bullet holes and damage caused by an artillery shell.

The Gettysburg Hotel was established in 1797 and is located across the street from the historic Will's House, where President Lincoln stayed and finished the Gettysburg Address. It offers shelter at a reasonable price and contains McClelland's Tavern, a good place to obtain nourishment and replenish your fluids. The Dobbin House Tavern (est. 1776), which has a secret "underground railroad" slave hideout, is another place where the authors have taken some comfort. The Farnsworth House offers Ghost Tours and a bookstore with many publications of local interest. We also stopped for a pint at O'Rorkes Eatery and Spirits on Steinwehr Avenue.

14.

HERMAN HAUPT

That Man Haupt . . .

County: Montgomery • Town: Bala Cynwyd
Buried at West Laurel Hill Cemetery
227 Belmont Avenue

> "That man Haupt has built a bridge four hundred feet long and one hundred feet high, across Potomac Creek, on which loaded trains are passing every hour, and upon my word, gentlemen, there is nothing in it but cornstalks and beanpoles." *—Abraham Lincoln, discussing Haupt's timely repairs to the Potomac Creek Bridge after the Battle of Fredericksburg, May 28, 1862.*

Herman Haupt was born in Philadelphia, Pennsylvania, on March 26, 1817. He was the son of Jacob Haupt, a merchant by trade, and Anna Margaretta Wiall Haupt. His father died when Herman was only 12 years old, leaving widow Anna to support her three sons and two daughters.

A child engineering prodigy, he was appointed to the United States Military Academy at only 14 and graduated at the age of 18 with the 1835 class (ranked 35th out of 56). Upon graduation, he was commissioned a second lieutenant in the 3rd U.S. Infantry but resigned his commission a couple of months later to become a civil engineer. In 1838, he married Ann Cecelia Keller in Gettysburg, Pennsylvania, with whom he had seven sons and four daughters.

Before the Civil War, Haupt worked primarily in the railroad industry as an engineer designing bridges and tunnels. He patented a bridge construction technique known as the "Haupt Truss." For most of the 1840s,

Herman Haupt

he was a professor of mathematics and engineering at Pennsylvania (now Gettysburg) College, before returning to the railroad industry.

Early in 1862, the second year of the Civil War, Secretary of War Edwin M. Stanton appointed Haupt chief of all U.S. military railroads and transportation, with the rank of colonel, serving under General Irvin McDowell, who was responsible for the defense of Washington, D.C.

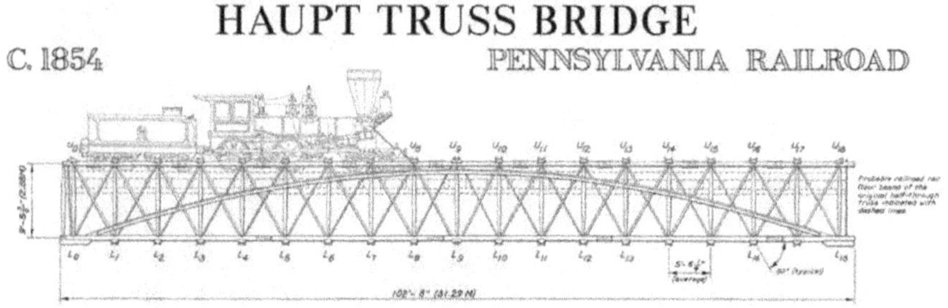

Haupt repaired damaged rail lines, built bridges, and improved telegraph communications.

On September 5, 1862, Haupt was promoted to brigadier general of volunteers. He refused the appointment but was willing to serve without rank or pay. He did not enjoy the protocols of military service and wanted the freedom to continue working in private business. The offer was officially rescinded one year later, in September of 1863, at which time he left the military.

However, during his year of service, he made an enormous impact on the Union war effort, being one of the few experts in the nation at that early time who understood the functioning of railroads and their value to the military. He assisted the Union Army of Virginia and the Army of the Potomac in the Northern Virginia and Maryland Campaigns. He was particularly effective in supporting the Gettysburg Campaign, conducted in an area he knew well from his youth. His hastily organized trains kept the Union Army well supplied, and he organized the returning trains to carry thousands of Union wounded to hospitals.

Haupt was known to show up at the war front or the White House at critical points in the war—like at George McClellan's headquarters just after the Second Battle of Bull Run, and at Joseph Hooker's headquarters before Lee invaded Maryland. Haupt also visited Fredericksburg shortly after the battle there in December 1862. According to Haupt biographer James A. Ward, "That evening Haupt and Congressman John Covode called on Lincoln in Washington to present firsthand reports of the

Excavating for "Y" at Devereux Station, Orange & Alexandria Railroad. The locomotive, General Haupt *is being used for work detail. Standing on the bank is USMRR Supt. for the O & A railroad, John Henry Devereux, who reported to General Haupt.*

battle. Haupt's account so upset the president that the three men walked at once to Halleck's house to confer on future action."

While on his way to Gettysburg, during a stop in Harrisburg, Haupt observed to a subordinate about the coming conflict: "We are in the most critical condition we have been in since the war commenced, and nothing but the interposition of Providence can save us. If the army is destroyed, no new force can be collected in time to make effectual resistance. Washington, Baltimore, Philadelphia, and New York will fall, and the enemy can then, as masters of the situation, dictate their own terms."

Haupt was extremely disappointed with General Meade's unwillingness to pursue Lee's army after Gettysburg. Said Haupt on July 5, 1863, to Meade, who was sure the Confederates' retreat would be slowed by

USMRR engine General Haupt

the lack of bridges: "Do not place confidence in that. I have men in my Construction Corps who could construct bridges in forty-eight hours sufficient to pass that army, if they have no other material than such as they could gather from old buildings or from the woods, and it is not safe to assume that the enemy cannot do what we can."

After this meeting, around midnight, Haupt jumped on a locomotive and rushed to Washington. Before breakfast, he showed up at President Lincoln's office. According to historian Fletcher Pratt:

> "On July 6 came Haupt in person to the White House, direct from the front, and officers with eyewitness accounts of the battle, including General Daniel Sickles, who had had a leg shot off on the second day. Haupt was no more comforting than Meade's order; he had seen the General the day before to tell him that the new railhead and telegraph had been carried

> through Hanover Junction to Gettysburg (which surprised Meade very much), and to plead with him to follow the enemy hard. Meade replied that his men needed rest; Haupt told him they could not be as tired as the Confederates: 'You must pursue Lee and crush him. His ammunition and stores must be exhausted, and his supply trains can be easily cut off. He is in desperate straits, like a rat in a trap, and you can whip and capture him'."

Upon hearing this report, Lincoln asked of Stanton, "What shall we do with your man, Meade, Mr. Secretary?"

"Tell him," said Stanton to Haupt, "Lee is trapped and must be taken."

Then Stanton turned to Lincoln and added, "He can be removed as easily as he was appointed if he makes no proper effort to end this war now, while he has Lee in a trap."

Haupt then hastened back to Gettysburg by train, expecting the orders from Washington would be obeyed. He offered his help, but Meade did nothing, thereby allowing Lee to escape. This greatly disappointed Lincoln, Stanton, and Halleck, and frustrated Haupt. If Meade had acted, or if anyone had thought to place Haupt in command on Sunday, July 5, 1863, Lee would doubtless have been captured, and the war ended.

Said Robert Lincoln, the President's son, about one of his visits to the White House in mid-July 1863:

> "Entering my father's room right after the battle of Gettysburg, I found him in tears with his head bowed upon his arms resting on the table at which he sat. 'Why, what is the matter, father?' I asked. For a brief interval, he remained silent, then raised his head, and the explanation of his grief was forthcoming. 'My boy,' he said, 'when I heard that the bridge at Williamsport had been swept away, I sent for General Haupt and asked him how soon he could replace the same. He replied, 'If I were uninterrupted, I could build a bridge with the material there

within twenty-four hours, and Mr. President, General Lee has engineers as skillful as I am.' Upon hearing this, I at once wrote Meade to attack without delay, and if successful to destroy my letter, but in case of failure to preserve it for his vindication. I have just learned that at a council of war of Meade and his generals, it has been determined not to pursue Lee, and now the opportune chance of ending this bitter struggle is lost."

Haupt's grave

After his war service, Haupt returned to the railroad business. He and his wife purchased a small resort hotel at Mountain Lake in Giles County, Virginia. He invented a prize-winning drilling machine and was the first to prove the practicability of transporting oil in pipes. Haupt became wealthy from his investments in railroads, mining, and real estate. Still, he eventually lost most of his fortune due to political complications involving the completion of the Hoosac Tunnel in Massachusetts.

Herman Haupt died of a heart attack at age 88, on December 14, 1905, in Jersey City, New Jersey. He was stricken while traveling by train on a journey from New York to Philadelphia. He is buried in West Laurel Hill Cemetery in Bala Cynwyd, Pennsylvania. He outlived every one of his West Point classmates.

If You Go:

West Laurel Hill Cemetery is a large, beautiful cemetery filled with history and exciting stories. It is home to the graves of eight Civil War Medal of Honor recipients, including George Stockman, Elwood Williams, Wallace Johnson, Richard Binder, Jacob Orth, Joseph Corson, Charles Betts, and Moses Veale. Details of their service can be found in Chapter 35 (Medal of Honor Recipients).

Also buried at West Laurel Hill Cemetery is Francis Adams Donaldson, whose letters and correspondence during the war to his family were published in the book *Inside the Army of the Potomac: The Wartime Letters of Captain Francis Adams Donaldson.*

15.

GETTYSBURG NATIONAL CEMETERY

"Four score and seven years ago, our fathers brought forth on this continent a new nation, conceived in liberty, and dedicated to the proposition that all men are created equal.

Now we are engaged in a great civil war, testing whether that nation, or any nation so conceived and so dedicated, can long endure. We are met on a great battlefield of that war. We have come to dedicate a portion of that field, as a final resting place for those who here gave their lives that that nation might live. It is altogether fitting and proper that we should do this.

But, in a larger sense, we cannot dedicate—we cannot consecrate—we cannot hallow—this ground. The brave men, living and dead—who struggled here, have consecrated it far above our poor power to add or detract. The world will little note, nor long remember what we say here, but it can never forget what they did here. It is for us the living, rather, to be dedicated here to the unfinished work which they who fought here have thus far so nobly advanced. It is rather for us to be here dedicated to the great task remaining before us—that from these honored dead we take increased devotion to that cause for which they gave the last full measure of devotion—that we here highly resolve that these dead shall not have died in vain—that this nation, under God, shall have a new birth of freedom—and that government of the people, by the people, for the people, shall not perish from the earth."

Bronze bust of Lincoln at the Gettysburg National Cemetery near the site of the Gettysburg Address (photo by Tammi Knorr)

President Abraham Lincoln's now immortal words were spoken at Gettysburg, Pennsylvania, on November 19, 1863, as part of the consecration of the new Soldiers' National Cemetery (now most often commonly referred to as the "Gettysburg National Cemetery," located a mile or so south of Gettysburg's town square with an east or "front" entrance off of Baltimore Pike and a west entrance off of Taneytown Road). Oddly

Rows at the Gettysburg National Cemetery (photo by Tammi Knorr)

enough, Lincoln was not even the featured speaker that day. One of the great orators of the time, Edward Everett from Massachusetts, mesmerized the crowd for two hours before Lincoln took the podium and, in a somber delivery, spoke for approximately two minutes.

Said Everett in a letter to Lincoln written shortly afterward, "I should be glad if I could flatter myself that I came as near to the central idea of the occasion, in two hours, as you did in two minutes." Lincoln replied he was glad to know the speech was not a "total failure."

Pennsylvania Governor Andrew Curtin, who sat on the speakers' platform that day, was pleased with the speech. He said of Lincoln, "He pronounced that speech in a voice that all the multitude heard. The crowd was hushed into silence because the President stood before them . . . It was so impressive! It was the common remark of everybody. Such a speech, as they said it was!"

In contrast, eyewitness Sarah A. Cooke Myers recalled in a 1931 interview, "I was close to the President and heard all the Address, but it seemed short. Then there was an impressive silence like our Menallen Friends Meeting. There was no applause when he stopped speaking." Historian Shelby Foote, in his book *The Civil War, A Narrative. Vol. 2: Fredericksburg to Meridian*, described the applause as delayed, scattered, and "barely polite."

Large statue of General John Reynolds at the entrance to Gettysburg National Cemetery (photo by Tammi Knorr)

One of the many rows of unknown graves (photo by Tammi Knorr)

Likely, the crowd probably was not expecting such a short speech from the president, especially after Everett's long one. The fact that the photographers in attendance were unable to get a good picture of Lincoln that day further confirms the brevity of the remarks and the likely lack of preparedness among those gathered. Of course, none of this detracts from the importance of the moment, especially when looking back many years later. What more could or should someone say on such an occasion? Since then, many have said that Lincoln's speech was one for the ages.

Lands, in general, can be sanctified in several different ways. One way is for something of momentous significance in human history to have transpired at a place. Without a doubt, the Gettysburg National Cemetery is the epitome of that type of sacred space. The final resting place of those buried here—in the very soil on which the three-day, turning-point-of-the-war battle occurred—makes these graves a collection of "Keystone Tombstones" unlike any other. Moreover, given the extreme significance of both the Battle of Gettysburg and the Civil War, this multi-thousand-acre site has served and will continue to serve as arguably the most important and enduring forum through which generations of Americans have held on to and grappled with their collective memories of the events that took place here over 150 years ago. There are few cemeteries on American soil as hallowed as this one.

Today, Gettysburg National Cemetery remains an incredibly special place. As you enter the cemetery's front gate, you behold a well-landscaped park. A statue of Major General John Fulton Reynolds greets you. Reynolds was the highest-ranking soldier killed at Gettysburg. While he is not buried here, the life-sized bronze statue of him standing near the entrance beckons you in to walk among his fallen comrades. Gettysburg buffs will note this is not the first—nor the last—large statue of Reynolds one encounters in Gettysburg. (See Chapter 1 herein for a more detailed discussion of Maj. Gen. Reynolds.)

There is an excellent display of Lincoln's Gettysburg Address at the far end of the cemetery, near a pavilion about 50 yards east of the Taneytown Road gate. However, neither the display nor the pavilion is the exact spot from which Lincoln made his Address. The Soldiers National Monument, a large monument in the center of the park, is close to the actual location. However, some have said it was just over the fence in neighboring Evergreen Cemetery.

There are 3,564 Union soldiers buried in Gettysburg National Cemetery. Of those, 979 (more than one-fourth) are unknown. New York (867) and Pennsylvania (534) claim over half of the known fallen. The rest are from 16 other states. There are no Confederates buried within the confines of the National Cemetery (but some may be forever resting within just a stone's throw—see the *"If You Go"* section below). Regarding the thousands of Confederates who fell and were interred on the battlefield, the National Park Service web site (http://www.nps.gov/gett/faqs.htm) states:

> The southern dead were removed to cemeteries in North and South Carolina, Georgia, and Virginia between 1871 and 1873. Most of the Confederate dead were interred at Hollywood Cemetery in Richmond, Virginia, in a special section set aside specifically for the casualties of Gettysburg.

If You Go:

Adjacent to the National Cemetery is a 29.12-acre, private, historic, rural cemetery called Evergreen. Founded nine years before the Battle of Gettysburg, Evergreen Cemetery became the eponym for Cemetery Hill, a landform most noted as the keystone of the Union position during the epic battle. While visiting Evergreen, be on the lookout for the less-than-a-handful of Confederate soldiers that may or may not have their final resting places here. Also, consider paying homage to David Wills and Henry Louis Baugher, both of whom are buried at Evergreen and had important connections to the creation and dedication of the National Cemetery.

Wills' grave at Evergreen (photo by Tammi Knorr)

Wills, acting on behalf of Governor Curtin, was responsible for coordinating the creation of the cemetery. He was a prominent attorney in the area and was the one who sent an invitation to President Lincoln to make "a few appropriate remarks" at the dedication. Lincoln stayed at Wills's house on the square in downtown Gettysburg. A visit to the David Wills House, now a museum, is highly recommended. After visiting the Wills House, we also recommend a stop at The Pub and Restaurant on the square for some refreshments and nourishment.

Baugher's grave at Evergreen (photo by Tammi Knorr)

Baugher attended the Lutheran Theological Seminary in Gettysburg and became a minister. By 1863, he was the second president of Pennsylvania (now Gettysburg) College. He spoke immediately after Lincoln's Gettysburg Address and gave the formal benediction for the National Cemetery.

16.

OLIVER B. KNOWLES

An Unknown Hero

County: Philadelphia • Town: Philadelphia
Buried at Laurel Hill Cemetery
3822 Ridge Avenue

It is incredible how difficult it is to find information about Oliver Blatchy Knowles considering what he did in his short life. He entered the Civil War as a private at the age of 19 and ended the war four years later, a brevet brigadier general at the age of 23.

Knowles was born on January 3, 1842, in Philadelphia. His father, Levi Knowles, was a prominent flour merchant who was heavily involved in civic and charitable organizations in Philadelphia. Oliver quit high school after two years and joined his father's business. He was tall (6'2"), and through his love of horses, he developed into an excellent horseman. When the war broke out, 19-year-old Knowles was recruited by William Henry Boyd of Philadelphia. Boyd was raising a company of cavalry, which would become part of the First New York Cavalry (also called the "Lincoln Cavalry"). Boyd was a captain, and young Oliver Knowles became his orderly as he quickly established a reputation for dedication to his duty and for following orders. Their colonel was a man named Carl Schurz, a former German Revolutionary of 1848 and confidant of President Lincoln.

The Lincoln Cavalry saw its first combat at Pohick Church, Virginia, on July 22, 1861. It was a skirmish with Confederate cavalry, the first cavalry-against-cavalry action in the war. In the four years that followed, Knowles and the men of the Lincoln Cavalry never forgot the lesson of that first encounter: in a cavalry fight, the advantage is with the party that

Lee surrenders to Grant at Appamattox Court House, after which Knowles was promoted

moves first. Knowles performed so well that in September 1861, he was promoted to corporal.

In January 1862, he was promoted again to sergeant, and after the Peninsula Campaign, he received a commission as a second lieutenant. The Lincoln Cavalry saw action at Antietam and then spent much of the early part of 1863 pursuing the troops known as Mosby's Raiders, a cavalry battalion commanded by John "Gray Ghost" Mosby. Mosby's Raiders were known for their quick raids and disappearances.

In April 1863, Knowles was made a first lieutenant and took a furlough. He rejoined the regiment in Harrisburg just in time to participate in the Battle of Gettysburg.

In August 1863, after much of the First New Yorkers' enlistments expired, the 21st Pennsylvania Cavalry was formed and mustered in with Boyd as its colonel and Knowles as a major. The regiment was dismounted and served as infantry during the Overland Campaign in the spring of 1864. In June, at the Battle of Cold Harbor, Boyd was severely wounded, and Knowles took command of the regiment. He led the 21st in action during the siege of Petersburg. In October, the regiment was mounted

The grave of General Knowles

and acting as cavalry again, and Knowles was promoted to colonel. He was 22 years old.

Knowles led the unit in various actions around Petersburg and then was sent to participate in the Appomattox Campaign. They saw action at Dinwiddie Court House, Five Forks, Sayler's Creek, and Appomattox Court House, where Lee would surrender on April 9, 1865. In June, Knowles received a brevet to brigadier general of volunteers for gallant and meritorious service. He left the army in July and returned home to Philadelphia.

Oliver Knowles moved to Milwaukee, Wisconsin, where he was in the grain trade. He was stricken with cholera and died on December 6, 1866, less than a month before his 25th birthday. His remains were returned to Philadelphia and buried in Laurel Hill Cemetery. His gravestone reads:

He was:
Gentle, yet courageous
Firm, but magnanimous
Beloved by all

His name is on the 21st Pennsylvania Cavalry Regiment monument on the Gettysburg Battlefield.

If You Go:

There are numerous Civil War generals buried in Laurel Hill Cemetery. The following six were all at the Battle of Gettysburg:

- **Louis Francine:** fatally wounded in the Peach Orchard on July 2, 1863. The 7th New Jersey Infantry Monument on the Gettysburg battlefield stands on the spot where Francine was wounded.
- **Benezet Foust:** led the 88th Pennsylvania Infantry and was wounded on the first day of the battle.
- **William Painter:** was with Major General John Reynolds when Reynolds was killed on Day 1 (see Chapter 1).
- **John Hoffman:** led the 56th Pennsylvania Infantry, which was the first Union infantry regiment to participate in the battle.

• **Langhorne Wister:** assumed command of his brigade on Day 1, when the previous commander, Edmund Dana, was struck down.

• **George Alexander Hamilton Blake:** was a cavalry officer who served with distinction during the Gettysburg Campaign.

A stone's throw from Laurel Hill is St. James-the-Less Episcopal Churchyard, which contains the graves of several Civil War generals and heroes. Among them is Robert Morris, Jr., the great-grandson of Revolutionary War patriot and Declaration of Independence signer Robert Morris. Morris, Jr. was captured by Confederate forces at the Battle of Brandy Station in Virginia and died while imprisoned at the infamous Libby Prison in Richmond.

Also at St. James-the-Less Episcopal Churchyard are the graves of John Grubb Parke, a major general who led his troops in the assault and capture of Vicksburg and fought in the Battles of Knoxville, Petersburg, and Fort Stedman, Virginia; Benjamin Chew Tilghman, who commanded the 26th Pennsylvania Volunteer Infantry and later the 3rd United States Colored Troops; James Barnet Fry, who served as Provost Marshal General of the Union Army; and Medal-of-Honor recipient Anthony Taylor (see *Keystone Tombstones Civil War* Chapter 35) who was awarded the Medal of Honor for his actions at the Battle of Chickamauga.

Libby Prison in Richmond, Virginia

17.

REBELS AMONG US

Scattered across the Keystone State, you will find the occasional pocket of rebel graves. While John Clifford Pemberton's status as a general makes him arguably the most prominent Confederate soldier buried in Pennsylvania (see *Keystone Tombstones Civil War* Chapter 17), there are many more of lesser renown. Below are some of the sites:

HELLAM TOWNSHIP, York County

One grave that recently received a lot of attention is the Unknown CSA marker along the Susquehanna River in Hellam Township, York County. The site is 1.2 miles north of the Accomac Inn. According to contemporary accounts, the soldier was a Confederate cavalryman whose body washed up along the western riverbank in June 1863. It was surmised he was a rebel scout drowned while trying to ford the river near York Haven. The body was found and buried by locals. In 1972, Hurricane Agnes supposedly washed away some of the bones. A more recent marker was lost in 2011 when tropical storm Lee pounded the county. In early 2013, there was an effort to restore the marker. Over 100 people were present at the site for its rededication, including several people in period dress, according to the *York Daily Record.*

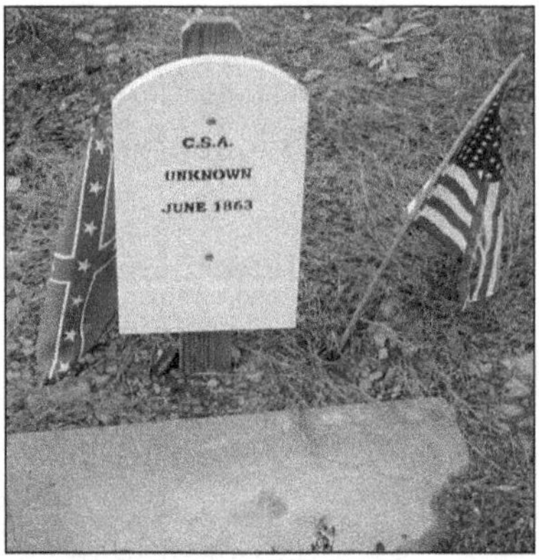

Temporary marker of Unknown CSA along the Susquehanna River in Hellam Township, York County (photo by Joe Farley)

PROSPECT HILL CEMETERY, York County

Many of the wounded soldiers from Gettysburg were transferred via train to York County. Some of those were Confederates who were not welcome to convalesce with the Union casualties. Instead, they were moved to Washington Hall, the meeting place of the local Odd Fellows Lodge on South George Street. Dr. Henry Nes, a known Southern sympathizer, was believed to be one of the physicians who cared for them. Five of the soldiers did not survive. They were taken by wagon to scenic Prospect Hill Cemetery, where they were interred. The grave is part of the Civil War walking tour of Prospect Hill Cemetery, an interesting stroll through York's Civil War history. A tour guide brochure is available at the gift shop of the York County Heritage Trust at 250 East Market Street (the historic Lincoln Highway) in downtown York. The tour guide discusses the Rebels, as well as scores of Civil War personalities also buried in the cemetery, including several Yankees mortally wounded at Gettysburg.

BIG MOUNT, PARADISE TOWNSHIP, York County

Imagine 4,000 Confederate troops showing up at your farm! That is precisely what was experienced on the evening of June 27, 1863, by George Jacob Altland and his immediate neighbors of Big Mount, Paradise Township, York County. General Jubal Early arrived and set camp here for the night. Somewhere in the Big Mount area, a farmer shot and killed Pvt. Charles Brown of the Louisiana Tigers, who was prowling around the region looking for food or supplies. Brown's service record reads "murdered by the citizens of York County, Pa." The grave is unmarked.

MANADA GAP CEMETERY, Dauphin County, PA

About 20 miles northeast of Harrisburg's Camp Curtin lay the graves of several Confederate soldiers who were prisoners of war—likely captured at Gettysburg. They were being used as laborers at the nearby Manada

Furnace, a local industry located along Manada Creek. The Grubb family, who owned the furnace, used prisoners as woodcutters to feed the busy furnace that produced many tons of pig iron. The soldiers lived nearby in wooden shacks and died during the war, most likely from disease. The marked burial site is only the best known. Up to a dozen more prisoners are buried near the original site of the workers' shacks, the stone foundations of which can still be seen. Additional Confederates are said to be buried near the Old Hanover Cemetery only a few miles away. All died during the war before they could be released to return home.

WEST LAUREL HILL CEMETERY, Bala Cynwyd

The following Confederate veterans are interred in West Laurel Hill Cemetery:

- **Captain John P. Donaldson, Jr.**, CSA (June 13, 1838–July 22, 1901): born and raised in Philadelphia, the son of John P. and Matilda Nice Donaldson. He was a descendant of the family for which the Nicetown section of Philadelphia was named. Donaldson's grandfather, William Donaldson, was Sheriff of Philadelphia from 1808 to 1810. Donaldson enlisted with the rebels in Charlestown, Virginia (now West Virginia), and saw action in several battles, receiving wounds at Droop Mountain and Gaines Farm.
- **Private William D. Mason,** CSA (December 7, 1846–October 22, 1909): the son of James W. Mason and Martha Cooke of Clarke County, Virginia. William married Louise "Lula" Clarke of Philadelphia. He enlisted at Brandy Station at age 15 and served one year until discharged for health reasons.
- **Private Frederick L. Pitts,** CSA (October 1842–1928): born in Berlin, Worcester County, Maryland. In 1861, he joined the Maryland Infantry at Richmond and fought throughout the war. After the war, Pitts studied art at the Pennsylvania Academy of Fine Arts in Philadelphia. He later was president of the Philadelphia Sketch Club, the oldest organization of artists in the United States. His art focused on marine subjects, as in his painting *The Wharf at Kaighn's Point.*

LAUREL HILL CEMETERY, Philadelphia

The following Confederate veterans are interred in Laurel Hill Cemetery:

• **Private George Lehman Ashmead,** CSA (December 15, 1837–December 15, 1898): served in Company E, 4th Texas Infantry Regiment, Hood's Texas Brigade. He died in Germantown, Philadelphia County, Pennsylvania.

• **Assistant Surgeon Fitz Henry Babbitt, MD,** CSA (December 29, 1829–February 14, 1909): born in Natchez, Mississippi, and graduated from the medical school of the University of Pennsylvania, class of 1853. He is believed to have served as a surgeon with a Louisiana Infantry Regiment between 1861 and 1864, according to their alumni register. The 1860 and 1870 census reports list him as a physician in Red River Landing, Pointe Coupee Parish, Louisiana.

• **Major Richard V. Bonneau,** CSA (April 26, 1827–January 27, 1899): the son of William Henry Bonneau and his wife, Anna Maria Swinton. He was born in Charleston, South Carolina. Richard was appointed to the Military Academy at West Point in 1847. He graduated in June 1852 and served on the frontier with the Third Infantry. On January 10, 1859, he married Marie Louise Kiehl in Philadelphia. She was the only daughter of John Kiehl and his wife, Jane Pickering. He returned to New Mexico and then resigned his commission to join the Confederacy at the outset of the war, serving until the end. He then returned to Philadelphia, where he entered the mercantile business with his father-in-law, John Kiehl. In his later life, Maj. Bonneau became a teacher and speaker in the Church of Christ.

• **Major General Samuel Gibbs French,** CSA (November 22, 1818–April 20, 1910): born in Mullica Hill, New Jersey. He was the son of Samuel French, Jr., and Rebecca Clark. French attended the U.S. Military Academy at West Point, graduating in 1843. Some of his West Point classmates were future Union Generals Ulysses S. Grant and William B. Franklin, as well as future CSA Generals Roswell Ripley and Franklin Gardner. French served bravely in the Mexican War. His first wife was Eliza Matilda Roberts of Philadelphia, who died in 1857. His second wife was a Southern woman. French resigned his commission in 1856 to become a Southern planter. When the Civil War started, he opted for his adopted South and became a brigadier general in the Confederate Army. His service first took him to the East, where he participated in the Peninsula Campaign and operations in North Carolina. Promoted to major general in August 1862, he was assigned to command a division in the Army of the Tennessee, leading his command in the Battles of Jackson, Atlanta, and Nashville. Illness forced him to return home in December 1864, but he soon returned to service commanding forces in Mobile, Alabama, until the end of the war. French spent the next 45 years of his life as a successful planter in Florida. He wrote an autobiographical account of his war services, entitled *Two Wars*. Though buried in Pensacola, Florida, a cenotaph stands here for him in his family's plot.

• **1st Lieutenant Henry A. Parr,** CSA, (ca. 1843–August 4, 1932): a cavalryman who became involved in the Confederate Secret Service. His actual place of birth is unknown—New York City, Nashville, and Nova Scotia are all possibilities. Parr joined General John Hunt Morgan's Raiders at the outbreak of the Civil War. Sometime in 1863, he began clandestine activities for the Confederate Secret Service. Along with Lieutenant John C. Braine, he helped to seize Union steamships in retaliation for former slave Robert Small's similar taking of the Confederate steamer USS *Planter* in 1862. Between 1863 and 1865, the officers and their crews hijacked the Union steamers *Chesapeake*, *Roanoke,* and the schooner *St. Mary's* at sea. After the war, Parr returned from exile in Nova Scotia, where he established a career as a pharmacist. In 1878, he became the last Confederate tried for war crimes for the murder of Chesapeake engineer Owen Schaffer. Parr was able to invoke the amnesty granted Confederate soldiers by President Andrew Johnson since he was working under the command of a duly commissioned Confederate officer, Braine. In 1884, Parr earned a dental degree from the prestigious Baltimore School of Dentistry, where he later became a clinical instructor. He became an expert in crowns and bridgework, often giving clinics at national dental meetings. He also held patents in non-dental fields. Dr. Parr died in New York City.

William Mason Turner

• **Surgeon William Mason Turner,** CSA/CSN (December 15, 1835–October 13, 1877): born in Petersburg, Virginia, he went on to graduate from Brown University in 1855 and the University of Pennsylvania Medical School in 1858. He began a medical practice in Petersburg, where he married Hannah Adelie Ford. With the outbreak of the Civil War, Turner joined the Confederate Army as a surgeon. In 1862, he resigned and was appointed an Assistant Surgeon in the Confederate Navy, where he served aboard the ironclad CSS *Chicora,* a Confederate gunboat stationed at Charleston, South Carolina. Turner also served in the naval battalion at Drewry's Bluff, Virginia. He was captured by Union forces in April 1865 and spent the last months of the war as a prisoner. After his parole, he resumed his medical practice in Philadelphia, where he became a regular contributor of poetry, prose, and medical literature to local publications. He also authored several dime novels for the Beadle & Adams publishing house. Turner died in Philadelphia.

• **Private George L. Washington,** CSA (January 12, 1825–February 7, 1872): born in Virginia, the great-grandnephew of President George Washington. During the Civil War, Washington enlisted in Col. John Mosby's Regiment of Partisan Rangers. On September 19, 1864, he was captured by Sheridan's forces at Winchester, Virginia. He remained a POW until paroled in 1865. Washington was married to Ann Bull Clemson, niece of the founder of Clemson University.

• **Private Phillip D. Woodhouse,** CSA: served with Company H, 16th Regiment, Virginia Infantry. His service records during the Civil War add up to an astonishing 119 pages. Private Woodhouse ended his wartime service as a hospital steward.

• **Private John Henry Zeilin,** CSA (December 25, 1834–December 20, 1896): served in the Confederate cavalry for Georgia and was a noted chemist, pharmacist, and president of J. H. Zeilin & Company, Philadelphia. Zeilin was the son of a prominent Delaware County (PA) attorney and register of wills, John K. Zeilin. As a teenager, Zeilin began a career in business at a Philadelphia drug firm. In 1853, he went south to work for Nottingham & Fitzgerald, a drug firm in Macon, Georgia. In 1861, he and a partner bought out his employer and established the J. H. Zeilin Company in the patent drug business in Macon.

During the Civil War, Zeilin was enlisted as a private in the Georgia Cavalry and was detailed to the staff of General Howell Cobb as a dispatch rider. He later was detailed to the CSA's Medical Department and assigned to procure medical supplies. After the war, Zeilin re-established his company in Philadelphia as a major patent drug manufacturer and distributor. One of its most popular products was Simmons' Liver Regulator. He married Emmeline Cole, daughter of Judge Carelton B. and Susan Cole of Macon, Georgia. Zeilin was also the nephew of Brigadier General Jacob Zeilin, 9th Commandant of the United States Marine Corps during the Civil War. He died of a stroke at Clifton Springs, New York.

NEW BRITAIN BAPTIST CHURCHYARD, New Britain

The following Confederate veteran is interred in the New Britain Baptist Churchyard:

• **Colonel Joseph Barbiere,** CSA (November 27, 1831–October 4, 1892), was born in New York City to Joseph and Flossie Ouvre Barbiere, who were natives of Marseilles, France. Joseph's grandfathers served in the American Revolution under General Lafayette and were at the British surrender at Yorktown. In 1850, Joseph, a lawyer, editor, and state trade representative, lived in Memphis, Tennessee, with his family. Barbiere married Mary Grey Levett in 1855. In 1860, they were

Col. Joseph Barbiere

recorded as living with her parents, Joseph and Eliza Levett, in New Britain, Pennsylvania, where his occupation was listed as "Gentleman." In 1861, Barbiere returned to Memphis, where he joined the Confederate Army. He was captured in April 1862 and prisoner-exchanged in the fall of 1862. He was then promoted and became an inspector general in the Confederate Army in Alabama. In 1864, he attained the rank of colonel in an Alabama unit known as Barbiere's Reserve Cavalry. After the war, Barbiere returned to Memphis and resumed his pre-war ventures as a trade representative. His wife, Mary, died in 1867 and is buried in Memphis. In 1868, Joseph married Mary's sister, Lucy Levett. By 1880, the Barbiere family had moved to Camden, New Jersey, where he worked as an editor. Later, they lived in Doylestown, Pennsylvania, for several years and then moved to Philadelphia. Barbiere wrote a book, *Scraps from the Prison Table at Camp Chase and Johnson's Island*, about his experiences as a prisoner of war. On one trade mission to France, Joseph became acquainted with a man who was attempting to invent a device that would transmit photographs across telephone lines. One of the earliest successes was the transmission between two cities of a photograph of Joseph Barbiere. He was given the reproduced photograph and brought it back to the United States, where it was donated to the Smithsonian Institution as one of the earliest existing examples of a fax. Barbiere died at his residence in Philadelphia.

MORRIS CEMETERY, Phoenixville

The following Confederate veteran is interred in Morris Cemetery:

• **Lieutenant Amory Coffin, Jr.,** CSA (August 9, 1841–June 5, 1916), was born in Charleston, South Carolina. Coffin was a cadet at the Citadel, class of 1861, in command of the squad, which fired the first shot of the Civil War, an alarm gun to notify the batteries around Charleston that the US Steamer *Star of the West* had been sighted and was bound for Fort Sumter. Coffin served at the Citadel throughout the war and was also an Assistant Professor of French and Drawing. Later appointed Adjutant. After the war, he joined the Phoenix Iron Company in Phoenixville. As a civil engineer with Phoenix, he designed the structural features of some of the late 19th and early 20th century's most famous buildings, including the Madison Square Garden in New York City, the Crocker Building in San Francisco, the Provident Life and Trust Company in Philadelphia, and others. Later, with noted architect George B. Post, he designed the steel structure of the New York Stock Exchange building. Coffin was elected to the American Society of Civil Engineers on March 3, 1875. He died in Scranton.

HOPE CEMETERY, Kutztown

The following Confederate veteran is interred in Hope Cemetery:

• **Colonel Thomas D. Fister,** CSN (October 25, 1838–April 21, 1915) was born in Kutztown, Pennsylvania. He graduated from the U.S. Naval Academy, class of 1859. When Louisiana seceded from the Union in January 1861, Fister was serving aboard the Revenue Marine Service Cutter *Robert McClelland.* Captain John G. Breshwood, the commander, turned his ship over to the State of Louisiana at New Orleans. A telegraphed message sent to Lieutenant S. B. Caldwell by U.S. Treasury Secretary John A. Dix ordered Caldwell to arrest Breshwood, and gave him the famous order, "If anyone attempts to haul down the American flag, shoot him on the spot." Lieutenants Caldwell and Fister did not carry out that order against their Captain. The *McClelland* was renamed the CSS *Pickens.* Breshwood, Caldwell, and Fister were dismissed from the Revenue Marine Service by order of the President and Treasury Secretary John A. Dix. Fister resigned his commission and joined the Confederate Navy. He survived the naval Battle of Fort Jackson and Fort Saint

Thomas Fister

Phillip, April 18-28, 1862, on the Mississippi River below New Orleans. His gunboat, the CSS *McCrae*, "riddled like a sieve" during the battle, transported the wounded to New Orleans under a flag of truce, then sank on April 27 at the New Orleans wharves. Fister escaped through the Union lines just after New Orleans fell to the Union Army. He made his way to Mobile, Alabama, and served on the CSS *Manassas* and CSS *Selma*. Later he commanded the naval brigade at Drewry's Bluff, Virginia, with the rank of colonel. After the war, Fister served in the Alabama legislature representing Calhoun County. He subsequently returned to Kutztown, Pennsylvania, with his wife, Julia L. Swan Fister, and family. He was a prominent citizen of Kutztown. Colonel Fister died in St. Paul, Minnesota.

ALLEGHENY CEMETERY, Lawrenceville

More than 250 Civil War soldiers and veterans are buried in the Soldiers Memorial Plot, including eight Confederates—most likely prisoners of war who did not survive their incarceration. Separated as they were in life from their white Union comrades, there are about 132 black Civil War veterans—members of the United States Colored Troops—who are buried about 30 yards away from the cluster of Union and Confederate graves.

EVERGREEN CEMETERY, Gettysburg

Two Confederates who were mortally wounded during the Battle of Gettysburg, Private Hooper Caffey, and Sergeant Matthew Goodson, were initially buried in Evergreen Cemetery. Due to public outrage, their remains were relocated to unmarked locations. The current markers are merely cenotaphs.

And what about the Confederate dead at Gettysburg?

Over 3,300 Confederate dead were buried in shallow graves and trenches at Gettysburg. Today, they are gone, having been returned to the South.

Confederate casualties at Gettysburg

Of these Confederate dead, 1,100 were buried in marked graves, and two Gettysburg residents, Dr. J.W.C. O'Neal and Mr. Samuel Weaver, recorded their locations. During the period October 27, 1863, to March 18, 1864, Weaver superintended the exhuming and removal of the Union dead to the Soldiers' National Cemetery at Gettysburg. He also, at that time, examined the graves of more than 3,000 Confederate dead. While examining the exhumed rebels, he was able to identify their remains by the burial locations, and then by the color, gray or brown, and the material (cotton) of the uniforms, the style of the shoes, and even by the undershirts, all of which were different than those of the Union soldiers. After the war, Ladies Memorial Associations contracted Weaver to remove and ship their lost soldiers south. Before the work could be started, however, Mr. Weaver died and his son, Dr. Rufus B. Weaver, took over the contract. Despite the many obstacles, including stubborn landowners, Rufus Weaver was able to complete the work.

18.

MEDAL OF HONOR RECIPIENTS

"A nation reveals itself not only by the men it produces but also by the men it honors, the men it remembers."

—President John F. Kennedy

Soldiers and Sailors Grove in Harrisburg (photo by Joe Farrell)

The Medal of Honor is the highest award for valor in action against an enemy force that can be bestowed upon an individual serving in the Armed Forces of the United States. The President awards the Medal of Honor in the name of Congress to a person who, while a member of the army or other service in the military of the United States, distinguishes himself or herself conspicuously by gallantry and intrepidity at the risk of his or her life above and beyond the call of duty while engaged in an action against an enemy of the United States, while engaged in an armed conflict against the opposing armed force in which the United States is not a belligerent party. The deed performed must have been one of personal bravery or self-sacrifice so conspicuous as to distinguish the individual above his comrades clearly and must have involved risk of life. Incontestable proof of the performance of the service will be exacted, and each recommendation for the award of this decoration will be considered on the standard of extraordinary merit.

In *Keystone Tombstones Volume I*, we visited and memorialized fifteen of Pennsylvania's Medal of Honor Recipients. The response from readers was extremely positive. In *Volume II*, we once again visited Medal of Honor Recipients everywhere we went and included eighteen in that volume. Along the way, we discovered that Pennsylvania honors its Medal of Honor recipients in Soldiers and Sailors Grove in Harrisburg. Located directly behind the State Capitol, the park serves as a memorial to all Pennsylvanians who have served in the U.S. armed forces. Included within the ribbon-like bands that represent various conflicts are the names of each Medal of Honor recipient for that conflict from Pennsylvania. Pennsylvania is second only to New York in the number of Medal of Honor recipients.

On the following pages are listed the Civil War Medal of Honor recipients buried in Pennsylvania.

• **Brest, Lewis,** Mercer Citizens Cemetery, Mercer. A private in Company D, 57th Pennsylvania Volunteer Infantry, Brest was awarded his CMOH for action he took in brutal hand-to-hand combat at the Battle of Sailors Creek, Virginia, on April 6, 1865. Before that time, Brest had an interesting combat history. Throughout 1862 and early 1863, he fought with his company and regiment in all the battles of the Army of the Potomac, including the Peninsular Campaign, Seven Days Battle, 2nd Bull Run, Fredericksburg, and Chancellorsville. Just before the Gettysburg Campaign, he contracted a severe case of typhoid fever, which kept him out of the battle (including his regiment's futile stand on Emmitsburg Road on July 2, 1863). Returning to his unit in late 1863 after his recovery, he served with them in Ulysses S. Grant's 1864 Overland Campaign and sustained a bullet wound in his neck during the Battle of the Wilderness. He recovered quickly from that injury and was present during the Siege of Petersburg from June 1864 to April 1865. It was during the final Union push against the Army of Northern Virginia that he captured a Confederate battle flag, garnering him a CMOH. His citation reads simply: *Capture of flag.*

• **Carlisle, Casper R.**, Mount Lebanon Cemetery, Mount Lebanon. A private in the Union Army in the Independent Pennsylvania Light Artillery, Carlisle was awarded the Medal of Honor for action on July 2, 1863, at Gettysburg, Pennsylvania. His citation reads: *Saved a gun of his battery under heavy musketry fire, most of the horses being killed and the drivers wounded.*

• **Clopp, John E.**, Lawnview Cemetery, Rockledge. A Private in Company F, 71st Pennsylvania Infantry, Clopp was awarded the CMOH for action on July 3, 1863, at Gettysburg, Pennsylvania. His citation reads: *Capture of flag of 9th Virginia Infantry (C.S.A.), wresting it from the color bearer.*

• **Collis, Charles Henry Tucky,** Gettysburg National Cemetery, Gettysburg. Collis was serving as Colonel of the 114th Pennsylvania Infantry at Fredericksburg, Virginia, on December 13, 1862, when he earned the Medal of Honor. His citation reads: *Gallantly led his regiment in battle at a critical moment.* He was subsequently a colonel of the 118th Pennsylvania Infantry at the Battle of Gettysburg. After the war ended, he moved to Gettysburg and established his residence there, and hence is buried in the Gettysburg National Cemetery (his grave is adorned with a monument that includes a bronze bust).

• **Furman, Chester S.**, Old Rosemont Cemetery, Bloomsburg. A corporal in Company A, 6th Pennsylvania Reserves, Furman was awarded the CMOH for his bravery during the second day of the Battle of Gettysburg, Pennsylvania (July 2, 1863). His citation reads: *Was 1 of 6 volunteers who charged upon a log house near Devil's Den, where a squad of the enemy's sharpshooters were sheltered, and compelled their surrender.*

• **Gilligan, Edward Lyons,** Oxford Cemetery, Oxford. A first sergeant in Company E, 88th Pennsylvania Infantry, Gilligan was awarded the Medal of Honor as for action on July 1, 1863, at Gettysburg, Pennsylvania. His citation reads: *Assisted in the capture of a Confederate flag by knocking down the color sergeant.*

• **Huidekoper, Henry Shippen,** Greendale Cemetery, Meadville. The Lieutenant Colonel and commander of his unit, the 150th Pennsylvania Volunteer Infantry, Huidekoper was awarded the CMOH for his bravery on the first day of the Battle of Gettysburg (July 1, 1863). He had commanded a portion of the 150th Pennsylvania in the initial heavy fighting around McPherson's Farm northwest of the town. When the 150th's Colonel, Langhorne Wister, took over command of the brigade, Lt. Colonel Huidekoper assumed command of the regiment. He then sustained a severe arm wound that eventually cost him his arm. He continued to direct his regiment despite the wound until the loss of blood forced him to retire; his remaining in the battle proved invaluable since every officer of the regiment had been killed or wounded. His citation reads: *While engaged in repelling an attack of the enemy, he received a severe wound of the right arm, but instead of retiring, he remained at the front in command of the regiment.* After the war, he served as a major general of the Pennsylvania National Guard and was active in suppressing the 1877 Labor Riots. He also served as Postmaster of Philadelphia, Pennsylvania, from 1880 to 1885, and was responsible for increasing the standard weight for mailing a letter from a half-ounce to an ounce.

• **Johnson, Wallace W.**, West Laurel Hill Cemetery, Bala Cynwyd. A sergeant in Company G, 6th Pennsylvania Reserves (35th Pennsylvania Volunteer Infantry), Johnson was awarded the CMOH for his bravery at the Battle of Gettysburg, Pennsylvania (July 2, 1863). His citation reads: *With five other volunteers gallantly charged on a number of the enemy's sharpshooters concealed in a log house, captured them, and brought them into Union lines.*

• **Mears, George W.**, Old Rosemont Cemetery, Bloomsburg. A sergeant in Company A, 6th Pennsylvania Reserves, Mears was awarded the CMOH for his bravery during the second day of the Battle of Gettysburg, Pennsylvania (July 2, 1863). His citation reads: *Was 1 of 6 volunteers who charged upon a log house near Devil's Den, where a squad of the enemy's sharpshooters were sheltered, and compelled their surrender.*

• **Miller, William E.**, Gettysburg National Cemetery, Gettysburg. The Captain in command of Company H, 3rd Pennsylvania Volunteer Cavalry, Union Army, Miller exhibited bravery on the third day of the Battle of Gettysburg, Pennsylvania, July 3, 1863, that would garner him a CMOH. That day, Captain Miller—on his own and without orders—led a charge upon a Confederate East Cavalry Field position with a squad of four troopers from his company. In this attack, he cut off and dispersed the enemy to the rear of his column. For this gallantry in the face of the enemy, he was awarded the Medal of Honor. His citation reads: *Without orders, he led a charge of his squadron upon the flank of the enemy, checked his attack, and cut off and dispersed the rear of his column. After the war, he served as a member of the Pennsylvania State Senate.*

• **Mulholland, St. Clair Augustin,** Old Cathedral Cemetery, Philadelphia. The Colonel and commander of the 116th Pennsylvania Volunteer Infantry (which was part of the famed "Irish Brigade"), Mulholland took part in the Battles of Antietam, Fredericksburg, Chancellorsville, and Gettysburg. He was awarded the CMOH for his bravery at the Battle of Chancellorsville (May 3-4, 1863), while Major of the 116th PA. His citation reads: *In command of the picket line held the enemy in check all night to cover the retreat of the Army.* His Medal was issued March 26, 1895. He is interred in an unmarked tomb that does not indicate either his status as a Brevet General or a CMOH recipient.

• **Reisinger, James Monroe,** Greendale Cemetery, Meadville. A corporal in Company C of the 150th Pennsylvania Volunteer Infantry, Reisinger performed heroically and bravely during the fight around McPherson's Farm on the first day of the Battle of Gettysburg (July 1). Those actions would garner him a CMOH, the citation for which reads simply: *Specially brave and meritorious conduct in the face of the enemy.* When his medal was awarded to him on January 25, 1907, he was the last of the sixty-three Union soldiers and officers to be issued the Medal of Honor for bravery at Gettysburg.

• **Roush, J. Levi,** Saint Patricks Cemetery, Newry. A corporal in Company D, 6th Pennsylvania Reserves (35th Pennsylvania Volunteer Infantry), Roush, and five of his fellow soldiers were awarded the CMOH for bravery on the 2nd day of the Battle of Gettysburg (July 2, 1863). His citation reads: *Was one of six volunteers who charged upon a log house near the Devil's Den, where a squad of the enemy's sharpshooters were sheltered, and compelled their surrender.*

• **Rutter, James May,** Hollenback Cemetery, Wilkes-Barre. A sergeant in the Union Army in Company C, 143d Pennsylvania Infantry, Rutter was awarded the Medal of Honor for action on July 1, 1863, at Gettysburg, Pennsylvania. His citation reads: *At great risk of his life went to the assistance of a wounded comrade and, while under fire, removed him to a place of safety.*

• **Sellers, Alfred Jacob,** Mount Vernon Cemetery, Philadelphia. He was a brevet colonel in the Union Army. He was awarded the Medal of Honor as a major in the 90th Pennsylvania Infantry for action on July 1, 1863, at Gettysburg, Pennsylvania. His citation reads: *Voluntarily led the regiment under a withering fire to a position from which the enemy was repulsed.*

• **Vanderslice, John Mitchell,** Saint James Perkiomen Church Cemetery, Evansburg. A private in Company D, 8th Pennsylvania Volunteer Cavalry, and first wounded at the June 1864 Battle of Cold Harbor, Vanderslice would go on to be awarded the CMOH for his bravery at the February 6, 1865, Battle of Hatcher's Run, Virginia. His citation reads: *Was the first man to reach the enemy's rifle-pits, which were taken in the charge.* After the war, Vanderslice was very active in Veterans' affairs; he sat in on the executive committee for the Gettysburg Battlefield Memorial Commission for seventeen years, and it was on his suggestion that states erect monuments to mark the positions on the battlefield where the individual regiments fought.

Sources

Books & Journals:

Catton, Bruce. *Mr. Lincoln's Army: The Army of the Potomac*. New York: Doubleday and Co, 1951.

———. *Glory Road; The Bloody Route from Fredericksburg to Gettysburg*. Doubleday, 1962.

———. *A Stillness at Appomattox*. Garden City, NY: Doubleday, 1954.

Dunkelman, Mark H. *Gettysburg's Unknown Soldier: The Life, Death, and Celebrity of Amos Humiston*. Westport, CT: Praeger, 1999.

Foote, Shelby. *The Civil War: A Narrative*. 2010.

Freeman, Douglas Southall. *Lee's Lieutenants: A Study in Command*. New York: C. Scribner's Sons, 1945.

Grow, Matthew J. *Liberty to the Downtrodden: Thomas L. Kane, Romantic Reformer*. New Haven: Yale University Press, 2009.

Guelzo, Allen C. *Gettysburg: The Last Invasion*. New York: Vintage Books, 2014.

Jordan, David M. *Winfield Scott Hancock: A Soldier's Life*. Bloomington, IN: Indiana University Press, 1995.

Krumwiede, John F. *Disgrace at Gettysburg: The Arrest and Court-Martial of Brigadier General Thomas A. Rowley, USA*. Jefferson, NC: McFarland & Co, 2006.

Longacre, Edward G. *General John Buford*. Cambridge, MA: Da Capo Press, 2003.

McPherson, James M. *Battle Cry of Freedom: The Civil War Era*. New York: Oxford University Press, 2003.

Miller, Francis Trevelyan, and Robert S. Lanier. *The Photographic History of the Civil War*. New York: Review of Reviews, 1911.

Miller, Jr., Arthur P. & Marjorie L. Miller. *Pennsylvania Battlefields and Military Landmarks*. Mechanicsburg, PA: Stackpole Books, 2000.

Millett, Allan R. & Peter Maslowski. *For the Common Defense: A Military History of the United States of America*. New York: The Free Press, 1984.

Nichols, Edward J., and John F. Reynolds. *Toward Gettysburg*. University Park: Pennsylvania State Univ. Press, 1958.

Sandburg, Carl. *Abraham Lincoln*. New York: Dell Pub, 1959.

Sears, Stephen W. *Gettysburg*. Boston: Houghton Mifflin, 2004.

Shaara, Michael. *Killer Angels*. New York: Ballantine Books, 1996.

Silverman, Kenneth. *Lightning Man: The Accursed Life of Samuel F.B. Morse*. Cambridge: Da Capo Press, 2004.

Small, Cindy L. *The Jennie Wade Story: A True and Complete Account of the Only Civilian Killed During the Battle of Gettysburg*. Gettsyburg, PA: Thomas Publications, 1991.

Smith, Timothy H. *John Burns: The Hero of Gettysburg*. Gettysburg: Thomas Publications, 2000.

(Audio Course)

Gallagher, Gary W. *The American Civil War.* Chantilly, VA: The Teaching Company, 2000.

(Films)

Gettysburg. Directed by Ronald F. Maxwell. Atlanta: Turner Pictures, 1993.
The Civil War. Directed by Ken Burns. Walpole, NH: Florentine Films, 1990.

Online Resources:

Ancestry.com – Family tree information and vital records.
FamousAmericans.net – for information on many individuals.
FindaGrave.com – for burial information, vital statistics, and obituaries.
Newspapers.com – Hundreds of newspaper articles were accessed—too numerous to mention here.
TeachingAmericanHistory.com – for information on many individuals.
TheHistoryJunkie.com – for information on many individuals.
Thoughtco.com – John Burns, Civilian hero of Gettysburg.
USHistory.org – for information on many individuals.
Wikipedia.com – for general historical information.

Index

www.ingramcontent.com/pod-product-compliance
Lightning Source LLC
LaVergne TN
LVHW091221080426
835509LV00009B/1110
* 9 7 8 1 6 2 0 0 6 4 5 2 8 *